Praise For

LIFE IN THE SEASON OF DYING

"In this sacred journal, Peter vulnerably shares 'riches stored in secret places'—intimate and holy moments with the dying, illuminating the promise of Psalm 116:15: 'His loved ones are very precious to him, and he does not lightly let them die.'"

—MOIRA BROWN, author, and former host of *100 Huntley Street*

"To pull life from death is a great calling upon the Christian community. Roebbelen's book does this honestly, beautifully, and with a compelling awareness that can only come from a hand that has held many in the journey towards death. I first read this while holding the hand of my sleeping mother, who is in her own season of dying. Having been absent, in a variety of ways, in the death of my father, I am now deeply grateful for a book that calls us (and shows us the way) to presence and life in the season of dying."

—GREG PENNOYER,
Editor of *God With Us: Rediscovering the Meaning of Christmas*

"An open, thoughtful discussion, not just about death, but the journey of life as we face the inevitability of death. This book calls us to live well so that dying well is possible. Most of all, it is an intimate insight to a pastor's heart—one who has walked openly with people he loved and cared about as they entered the mystery of dying. This is essential reading for anyone entering into the debates of a society fearful of death."

—DR. GARY V. NELSON, President, Tyndale University College and Seminary

"All of us are already somewhere on the journey toward dying. Whether you are enjoying abundant health or saying goodbyes, *Mercy* is a guide filled with intimate stories, shared with a shepherd's heart and overflowing with precious wisdom not just for dying well but for living well every day."

—DR. STEVE A. BROWN, President, Arrow Leadership, and
author of *Leading Me: Eight Practices for a Christian Leader's Most Important Assignment*

"Accompanying dying people is the most privileged part of pastoral ministry and also the toughest. This book's heartening testimonies demonstrate paradoxical gifts and blessings from the end of life. Discover how a dedicated pastor overcame fear of working with the dying and became an agent of God's healing and hope in the direst of circumstances."

—REV. ARTHUR PAUL BOERS, author of *Living into Focus: Choosing What Matters in an Age of Distractions*

"How do you help someone to die? Or those left behind? Realizing he had come up against his own limits as a pastor, Peter Roebbelen turns to the experience of those he has seen over the threshold. In their responses, he discovers what he calls the gifts of dying—which, when attended to, can transform the very way we live. Here is an honest account of a believer living at the edge of what we can understand in facing our own shared mortality."

—JERUSHA MCCORMACK, author of *Grieving, A Beginner's Guide*

"So often in the presence of death the Christian response is to pray for healing so life will continue. Turning that notion on its head, this book demonstrates that life and healing can actually be part of death both for those who are approaching the end of life on the earth as well as for those who are walking with them. But what is both disarming and helpful is that the author gives us a vulnerable glimpse into his own inner discovery around this complex subject, and in the process, invites readers to confront our own journey as we move toward death."

—DR. ROD WILSON, former President, Regent College, Vancouver, and co-author of *Keeping Faith in Fundraising*

"Although arguably the most important topic for us all, dying is never easy to discuss. Breathing life into personal stories of death is a wonderful way to engage others in dialogue. In *Mercy*, Roebbelen does just that, and with the imagery of acknowledging death's reality—not with our hands up in human submission, but instead with our '*palms up*' in Christian surrender."

—MEGORY ANDERSON, PHD, author of *Sacred Dying Journal: Reflections on Embracing the End of Life*

Peter Roebbelen

MERCY

LIFE IN THE SEASON OF DYING

PARACLETE PRESS
BREWSTER, MASSACHUSETTS

248.86
Roe

¹/18
B+

2018 First Printing

Mercy: Life in the Season of Dying

Copyright © 2018 by Peter Roebbelen

ISBN 978-1-61261-783-1

Library of Congress Cataloging-in-Publication Data

Names: Roebbelen, Peter, author.
Title: Mercy : life in the season of dying / Peter Roebbelen.
Description: Brewster, Massachusetts : Paraclete Press Inc., 2018. | Includes
    bibliographical references.
Identifiers: LCCN 2017043918 | ISBN 9781612617831 (trade paper)
Subjects: LCSH: Death—Religious aspects—Christianity.
Classification: LCC BT825 .R595 2018 | DDC 248.8/6—dc23
LC record available at https://lccn.loc.gov/2017043918

10 9 8 7 6 5 4 3 2 1

Published by Paraclete Press
Brewster, Massachusetts
www.paracletepress.com

Printed in the United States of America

TO SHARON, ERICA, AND JULIA
who keep showing me what it means to live abundantly.

TO MY DEAR FRIEND BOB,
whose spirit of grace, integrity, and kingdom still guides me.

CONTENTS

INTRODUCTION

WゝHEN I BECAME A PASTOR NEARLY 30 YEARS AGO, no one warned me about death and dying. Nobody told me I would watch so many friends die. During one particularly difficult decade, the deaths came in waves. As one wave overwhelmed me emotionally and spiritually, I barely had time to get my head above water and catch my breath before I saw the next wave cresting towards me. I spent weeks, months, and years walking with dear friends, helping them to grieve, and in the process, I did not grieve well. Though I encouraged them to cry, I rarely did. In helping them to die well, I seemed to be living poorly. The weight of sadness darkened my soul.

During a life-giving sabbatical, I began to work through my losses, trying to make sense of all the specific and personal deaths, but also death in general. I needed healing for my own journey of grief and also longed for understanding.

Why does a 43-year-old husband and father of two die after a three-and-a-half-year battle with ALS? Why does a 57-year-old woman suffer through 18 years of cancer treatments and finally succumb, leaving daughters, a grandchild, parents, and siblings? Why does a three-year-old fall off a dock and drown? Why does a 43-year-old mother of three contract an exceedingly rare form of brain cancer that claims her life within two years of discovery? Why do parents have to bury their only two children within six weeks of each other?

Even now the thought of these events disorients me, short-circuiting my understanding of life and faith. As I write about these experiences, I join a large group of men and women who have, through the years, tried to make some sense out of death, an event most commonplace, yet shocking in its ruthless and disturbing randomness.

Rethinking death is especially challenging since the subject dominates much of our interior landscape as well as our culture. Books, movies, TV shows, and news all incorporate death as a major theme and focus. We are fascinated and frightened by death in general while simultaneously finding it virtually impossible to come to grips with our own mortality. To have a healthy, mature, and truthful understanding of death is rare—except, perhaps, amongst the dying.

As we struggle with death, we should not stop being sad or stop grieving over the loss of loved ones. No, not at all. But we should be clear about what our head tells our heart, even while our heart is breaking. A healthy emotional view of death will allow for a healthy emotional view of life. Preparing for a good death will result in living a good life. If we stop approaching the subject of death with fear, awkwardness, uncertainty, and denial, we can more fully participate in that abundant life God says is ours to have.

This book does not answer the really hard questions such as what happens at the moment of death, or what is heaven like, or the most difficult question of all: why? In fact, this is not an answer book at all. It is much more a book of discovery.

During my time of grieving and reflecting, God showed me that every death has within it the possibility of new life. This is not a new thought. Jesus taught that every seed must die, that is, be buried in the ground, for new life to occur. Jesus predicted that out of his death much good would come. But we rarely focus on new life during a season of grief. Our pain often blinds us to all that is really happening. We do not look for signs of life and, therefore, we do not see them.

While this was a much-needed reminder for me, the more significant discovery was that the *journey* towards death, and not just the death itself, brought with it surprising gifts of life. God showed me that my dying friends were never more alive than in their season of dying. I glimpsed this new life on occasion, marveling at the grace and peace with which some of the dying faced their end; but God was showing me more than a courageous death. The dying were living better than I was. They were more fully alive, more fully present, more keenly aware of what was important and what was needed. This was an awareness that came upon me gradually, and my first response was an increased gratitude for God's mercy to the dying—for the many gifts of life I had not fully appreciated along the way. And then, I was humbled by the many gifts my dying friends were regularly giving to me—only some of which I caught in the moment.

As I journeyed with my dying friends, I held their hands, prayed for their healing, listened to their unanswerable questions, cried with them, counseled them a little and learned from them a lot. I continue to be in close relationship with many of their loved ones. These dead friends and surviving family members constitute a faithful "cloud of witnesses" (Hebrews 11-12) that continue to shape my understanding of dying and living. They bear witness to the pain and the unfairness of death but also to incredible grace and beauty, hope and courage, peace and surrender. They are a portal to the life God intends us to live. This book is filled with their stories, their wisdom, and their tears.

I am so very grateful for the permission to include these stories in this book. There would not be a book without them. Most of the people mentioned in this book, if they are still alive, have had a chance to review their stories. For those who have died, I have contacted family members for permission. In most cases, the names, dates, places, and events are meant to be accurate, but it is possible I have confused some of the details. In a few stories, where I have been unable to make contact with family members, I have changed the names and left out identifying details. As I journeyed with the dying, I heard and witnessed many things that are simply too personal and too holy to share.

There are many helpful books about the dying process and about coping with loss and what to expect as one journeys through grief. This is not one of those books. This book looks at the possibility of life in the face of death's certainty. With the dying and their caregivers showing the way, this is a book for hopeful living.

I cannot help bringing my worldview to the writing of this book. I experience the world as a follower of Jesus Christ. I believe a good and loving God incarnated himself in the fully human, fully divine Jesus. In a mysterious display of outrageous love, the perfect, sinless Jesus willingly died for our wrongdoings, so we might have the possibility of eternal life with the God who created us and continues to love us. This possibility is realized when we acknowledge our selfish and pride-filled ways, ask God for forgiveness, and commit our lives to honor and follow Jesus as the One who saves us from ourselves. One critical implication of this worldview is that those who die in Christ, that is, those who have chosen to honor and follow Jesus, look forward to new and eternal life both now and after physical death. Death is not the end. There is an ongoing heaven, and it is profoundly good. We have great confidence we will see God with our own eyes. This belief in God who loves us, Jesus who saves us, and eternity that awaits us is the grid through which I process my experiences with the dying. Those who believe physical death marks the complete end to their existence will, in all likelihood, view death (and life) quite differently.

The book you have in your hands did not start out to be a book. It started as journal entries, notes, scribbles, thoughts, and reflections as I took time to work through my own grief. As God brought a measure of healing to my heart and some new understanding to my mind, I began to wonder if others might be helped by my journey of death and discovery. I wondered if those facing their own death might find this to be a source of life and a source of hope. I wondered if caregivers and loved ones might see in these pages a new way of perceiving the death journey. I also hoped this might be an encouragement to those who are healthy, to those of us who appear to be in no imminent risk of dying—an encouragement to take a closer look at death and receive some guidance from the dying on how to live. This book is about finding life in the season of dying. One way to summarize this book might be to suggest this:

Loving well allows us to live well.
Living well prepares us to die well.
Dying well produces new life.

Although I include many stories from different death and dying experiences, there are a few deaths that have impacted me more deeply than others. I start with the story of Dave's death and end with Bob's death, and, in between, I mention these two men several times. It is not that their stories are more important than others but simply that Dave and Bob were close friends whose life and death continue to influence me. I think about them often.

The book is somewhat loosely organized around a series of gifts experienced by the dying and their caregivers. I speak of "gift" as a surprising act of grace bestowed upon the dying by God, who loves us deeply in life and death. Some of these gifts, such as peace, love, and simplicity, have an intuitive sense about them.

Others, such as dependence, time, and reverence, seem rather strange and require more explanation. The gifts are presented in chapters 2–19. The order in which they are presented, although not random, lacks any real significance. They are a collection of life-giving mercies bestowed upon the dying in ways that cannot be prescribed or predicted. They are, however, available.

The final few chapters are given to a somewhat broader exploration of death, including our almost universal fear of death, the danger of ignoring death, preparation for a good death, and the surprising life that continues to emerge in the midst of death.

I readily acknowledge there is much about death and dying, life and living that remains beyond my understanding. When friends lost their only son, I told them I did not understand why their son had died. In the face of inconsolable grief, there was much I did not know. Forty-four days later, these same parents laid to rest their only daughter. And in the midst of incomprehensible sorrow, I confessed to knowing even less.

That confession holds true today.

MERCY

LIFE IN THE SEASON OF DYING

ONE

Dave's Story

In September 1997, Lorie and Dave received the news Dave had ALS (Amyotrophic Lateral Sclerosis), also known as Lou Gehrig's disease, a motor neuron disease that causes the muscles to weaken and atrophy. Science and medicine know no cure. For the next three-and-a-half years, Dave and Lorie, their two daughters, Candace and Meghan, their extended family, and friends pitched battle against this devastating disease. Over those years, I became close friends with Dave and Lorie, gaining the privilege of walking with them in life's final journey. Although hard and painful, the journey was rich and full of life. Dave and Lorie, Candace and Meghan taught me much about loving and living and dying. So much so, I have yet to take it all in. Dave's spirit continues to bring me new life. The following account describes Dave's final days.

It was Sunday and Mother's Day. With our church service finished and the last of the equipment put away, I got into my car and headed home for lunch—a lunch I had planned and now needed to prepare for my wife and our two daughters. Dinner was also my responsibility that day, but we would never get that far. On the way home, a very anxious Lorie called me on my cell phone with the news that Dave was nonresponsive. Although he was still breathing, Lorie could not wake him up. He had gone to sleep as usual the night before but could not be roused even though it was now midday. We quickly decided Lorie should call an ambulance.

Before I got home, Lorie called again to tell me the ambulance was on its way. The cell phone rang for the third time, and Lorie, now in the ambulance with her husband, was clearly panicking. The paramedics had asked Lorie a question she was not prepared for: "Do you want us to take heroic measures?" The question exploded like a bomb in Lorie's head. She was not ready for Dave to die. Not like this. Although the battle had been long and draining, it felt as if death had just made a surprise appearance. Lorie and Dave were not finished with life quite yet. And so, we decided everything possible should be done to keep Dave alive.

When I arrived home and explained the situation to my wife, we both knew Mother's Day plans would have to wait. Soon I joined Lorie in the emergency room of Mississauga's Credit Valley Hospital. The staff worked hard to bring Dave back from the brink of death. They put a breathing tube down his throat and hooked him up to a respirator. They tested him for a number of possible causes for the sudden downturn. After two hours, they concluded the disease had simply progressed too far: Dave's breathing could no longer sustain his body. There would be no quick fix, no antibiotics, no treatments, no procedures. Dave was dying. The ALS had reached its final stage.

The rest of that day and Monday were painful, grueling days for Dave. With the help of the respirator, Dave regained consciousness. The respirator kept him breathing, but he could barely communicate, his discomfort clearly evident.

In the midst of these dark hours, something very comforting occurred. The community gathered to bear witness to life's greatest passage. Lorie, Candace, and Meghan were already at the hospital. But soon extended family members arrived, followed by Lorie and Dave's closest friends. And then it seemed like a dam burst somewhere, and the hospital corridors could no longer contain all the friends and neighbors and caregivers and work associates and even more distant relatives. They came to pray, to support, to love, to grieve, and to say good-bye. They brought emotional encouragement and spiritual strength. By their presence, they declared death should not be faced alone.

Dave's community took up residence in the large waiting area just outside the Critical Care Unit (CCU) where Dave lay dying. In the final 80 hours of Dave's life, members of the community were always present. They ebbed and flowed in numbers and in composition, but the community of care never disappeared. And the people came not just to watch a loved one die but also to encourage and support and embrace and to help in many practical ways.

The community brought with them a constant supply of food. Whenever Lorie, Candace, or Meghan left the CCU and reconnected with friends and family in the hallway, invariably they could choose from a never-ending supply of muffins, donuts, and cold drinks, but also full lunches and dinners. Multi-course meals for 10 to 15 people showed up regularly—a profoundly simple demonstration of practical love in action.

Some people came and stayed for days, some people came and stayed for minutes. The length of time did not matter—showing up did.

On Tuesday, Dave decided to go off the respirator in response to a powerful encounter with God in which God reassured Dave of his presence and said, "Trust me." Family and friends gathered around his bedside and we read a psalm and prayed, and then we held our collective breath as the doctor removed the tube from Dave's throat and turned off the machine. Dave, his voice raspy and weak, began to speak. He said, "I see a light." I thought, this is incredible—he's seeing Jesus coming to take him home. "I see a light," repeated Dave, "and it's right up there"—and he motioned to the ceiling light over his bed. Incredibly, it was a joke! When we realized Dave was playing with us, we all laughed. And with the laughter, the tension, anxiety, and fear all melted away. One moment we expected Dave to give up his spirit, to breathe his last, and the next moment we were laughing. How does that happen? How could we laugh when we had a dying man in our midst? Better still, why would a dying man, hardly able to speak, use his precious energy to make us laugh? I suspect he had the joke worked out long before he came off the respirator. Unbelievable.

Before long we were crying again. Within a few hours, Dave's diminished breathing caused him to slip back into a nonresponsive state—almost like a coma. We all thought the end had finally come. Lorie, Candace, and Meghan stayed by Dave's side throughout Tuesday night and into the next morning. Around 11 AM on Wednesday, with Dave hovering on the brink of death, we prayed, cried again, and said our good-byes to a body that quite frankly already looked dead. Only Dave's shallow breathing gave evidence he was still alive.

And then, incredibly, miraculously, Dave woke up. I don't know how else to say it. He simply *woke up*. I find it hard to describe what we experienced in that moment and in the following hours. It seemed as if the Spirit of God descended upon Dave and brought new life to his body. Dave's eyes began to sparkle. His breathing strengthened. His speech improved dramatically. And he was energized, fully alert. But even more dramatic than his renewed physical body was his renewed spirit. It seemed Dave's spirit had taken control of his decaying body and willed it back into action. We were awestruck by such a dramatic intervention from God.

When a man awakens from a deathlike coma, it is pretty exciting news. The nurses just shook their heads, bewildered and astonished. Someone called Dave's family doctor, and he rushed over and we stood there side by side, marveling at Dave's new life. The doctor said quietly, reverently, hopefully, "You know, it wouldn't surprise me if he got up and walked out of here."

News of Dave's "awakening" filtered out into the hospital corridors and waiting rooms and even further to friends and family members who, having said their final good-byes, had already returned home. His room filled with speechless loved ones who did not know what to think or do. Eventually, all but one returned to the waiting room to allow Dave some time with his wife and daughters. The one who stayed behind began to share that he no longer wanted to carry on his current lifestyle and was ready to begin a new life as a follower of Jesus. I can still see Dave's gaunt face stretched wide with the biggest, most beautiful smile. What a timely, precious answer to Dave and Lorie's many years of praying. In Dave's dying, Jesus brought new life. New life out of death— what a paradox.

In an incredible display of dying well, Dave spent the rest of that Wednesday encouraging and giving new life to others. He challenged many of his family and friends to a new or renewed faith in Christ. He encouraged us to live honorable and godly lives. Over an eight-hour period, Dave met with and spoke to every member of his family and Lorie's family and many of his closest friends. They would come to his bedside in small shifts, in twos and threes, and he had personal words of blessing and encouragement and challenge for each one. We received Dave's words, along with his remarkable alertness and energy, as a wonderful gift from God.

We, who had come as encouragers and supporters, we who had come as the hands and feet of Jesus, met Jesus in the one we had come to serve. We, the healthy, found ourselves ministered to by the dying. Perhaps Dave was the healthiest one of all that day.

As the afternoon moved into the evening, Dave's strength and our excitement began to fade. Lorie and I looked at each other with a quiet sense of knowing: the end was near. While the extended family and friends stayed out in the waiting area, Dave spent his final hours blessing and encouraging his wife and children. I have these images seared into my mind and heart as Dave, in the tradition of the Old Testament prophets, first blessed Candace and then Meghan and then Lorie. We stood on holy ground. Dave's inspired words conveyed his love and admiration and respect for each of his girls. He shared with them pictures of a special future. He told them over and over again how proud he was of them, and how much he loved them. He told them of his absolute assurance he would soon be in heaven. And he told them not to be angry with God. Dave spent the last hours of his life encouraging and giving peace to his family.

Dave's final hour was surreal. With Candace and Meghan holding his hands and with Lorie and me on either side of his head, and with his voice barely a whisper, Dave turned to Lorie and said, "Sing me home." And Lorie sang his favorite song. And then David turned to me and said, "Pray me home." And I prayed. And with my hand on his head, I reminded my dear friend he was the beloved son of God, he had fulfilled all his earthly duties, he was free to go, and he had blessed us beyond measure.

When Dave quietly slipped away around 9:15 on Wednesday evening, Lorie, Candace, and Meghan had done everything they could possibly do and had said everything that needed to be said. In the end, they did not flinch, they did not turn their heads or avert their eyes. Dave died with Lorie's kisses on his lips and with his daughters' hands in his hands.

Within minutes of Dave's passing, Meghan announced, through her tears, she could picture her Dad in heaven doing cartwheels, free from the body that had failed him, able to move without assistance, completely healed. In the final days, the community of care gave the Moreaus a little taste of heaven. In turn, quite unexpectedly, Dave gave us a taste of heaven as well. Dave's death continues to give me life.

I share Dave's story with you because it illustrates a number of the gifts described in the following chapters. My three-year journey with the Moreaus brought me great joy and deep grief. It was destabilizing, disorienting, and confusing. But Dave taught me so much. I didn't know at the time Dave's death was the first wave in a decade of deaths that would ultimately lead to the writing of this book.

In his letter to the Colossians, Paul describes God's intent for people who follow Jesus. Paul presents this desired end-state in the metaphor of putting on new clothes.

> Since God chose you to be the holy people he loves, you must clothe yourselves with tenderhearted mercy, kindness, humility, gentleness, and patience. Make allowance for each other's faults, and forgive anyone who offends you. Remember, the Lord forgave you, so you must forgive others. Above all, clothe yourselves with love, which binds us all together in perfect harmony. And let the peace that comes from Christ rule in your hearts. For as members of one body you are called to live in peace. And always be thankful. Let the message about Christ, in all its richness, fill your lives. Teach and counsel each other with all the wisdom he gives. Sing psalms and hymns and spiritual songs to God with thankful hearts. And whatever you do or say, do it as a representative of the Lord Jesus, giving thanks through him to God the Father.
> —Colossians 3:12–17, NLT

We put aside the old clothes of our former, immature, and self-centered lives and put on new clothes consistent with spiritual and emotional maturity. Within this metaphor, Paul presents a whole list of attributes, attitudes, and characteristics that are gifts from God—gifts we share with the world around us. Many of the dying have put on their new clothes while the rest of us are too busy and too preoccupied to bother changing.

Given that we will die, how then shall we live? Given that we will all face the death of loved ones, how shall we carry on?

The chapters that follow attempt to describe some of the new life, wisdom, and insights I discovered in my journey with the dying. But be warned, even the best of deaths remains painful and messy. The dying and those who love them often experience the journey quite differently. While I doubt I have captured all the life God brings to the dying, I fear even this partial list may cause further grief, pain, and, perhaps, guilt to some. You might wonder why your dying is not like those described in this book. My hope and sincere intent is not to add more pain but to share the possibility of experiencing life in the season of dying and, thereby, perceiving death in a new and life-giving way.

TWO

Dependence

Vicky was a fiercely independent, middle-aged woman who became a dear friend over the years. Her outlook on life was shaped by being raised in an emotionally barren family, by her own failed marriage that left her to raise two daughters on her own, and by her 18-year battle with cancer. Vicky was tough, but in the sweetest of ways. She was a lovely lady—generous, gracious, never asking for much, but always quick to lend a hand. Vicky did not complain about her pain—physical or emotional. During her numerous cancer flare-ups, her daughters and friends would repeatedly ask, "How are you doing?", to which she typically replied, "I'm doing okay. How are you?" She didn't like to talk very much about her visits to the doctors, the chemo and radiation treatments, or the constant concern about where and when the next spot would appear. And when friends asked, "Can we do anything to help?" Vicky would often reply, "I'm good for now. Thanks for asking." Vicky's sweet, gentle manner masked an emotional distance few could breach.

But Vicky changed. Slowly, the cancer began to chip away at the protective walls. Tears replaced the toughness. Giving gave way to receiving. In the final few years of her life, Vicky embraced the love and support of family and friends. Now she allowed them to get groceries, clean her apartment, and share in the emotion of her life-and-death struggle.

As the end neared, her daughter Nicole invited Vicky to live with her. I can still see the expression of joy and gratitude on Vicky's face when she told me about the invitation. Nicole provided a safe home for her mom. Both daughters, Nicole and Sarah, and several of Vicky's friends provided regular and ongoing care in her final months. Vicky passed away in her daughter's home in the loving embrace of family and friends. Vicky's move from stoic independence to grateful dependence benefited the caregivers as well, bringing them a measure of peace and contentment.

The dying experience huge loss—the loss of health, the loss of mobility, the loss of independence, the loss of doing simple everyday things. In the midst of this loss, the dying can experience the gift of dependence. Many would protest describing dependence as a gift. But we move off this earthly stage the same way we enter— in a state of complete dependence. When the dying accept their dependent state and allow others to care for them, they receive a profound gift that benefits both them and their caregivers. When friends, loved ones, volunteers, and professionals come alongside the dying in loving and compassionate ways, they awaken this wonderful life-giving gift in the dying. At the same time, when the dying allow us the privilege of caring for them, we receive much joy and fulfillment.

The sick and dying initially resist the journey towards dependence. Perhaps they believe dependence and weakness go hand-in-hand, and their pride prevents them from going down that road. Some see the struggle to remain independent as noble and heroic—a battle best fought to the bitter end. Unfortunately, this often results in resentment, anger, shame, and a sense of uselessness. The continued progression of their illness is felt as personal failure or as a deep disappointment in God and the medical system. This heroic battle only ever ends one way—in death. We have no choice in this. We will all surely die. We do, however, have a choice in how we die. Will we die with clenched fists railing against the unfairness of life? Or will we, with open hands, receive all the love that awaits us? As the dying accept the reality of their cumulative losses, they open themselves up to receive the love and compassionate care of others. Loss creates a huge hole in our heart, and it hurts a lot. But there is much love to fill that hole—if we allow it.

Henri Nouwen claims the first task in preparing oneself to die well is to become like a child again. He says entering a second childhood is essential to dying a good death.[1] Jesus said the same thing: "Unless you change and become like children, you will never enter the kingdom of heaven" (Matt. 18:3, NRSV). What does it mean to become like a child again? Many things, I suspect—wide-eyed wonder, innocence, absolute faith, but most of all, entering a new level of dependence. Children depend greatly (almost completely) on parents, teachers, and friends. In most cultures, the journey towards adulthood parallels the move towards independence. Then, when we get old or sick, we become increasingly dependent again. Apparently, Jesus sees this as a good thing and a requirement for entrance into the kingdom of heaven. One of the strongest images given for Christians in the Bible is that we are children (and heirs) of God.

Surrendering our lives completely comes with great struggle because it defies the natural order of things. We would much rather cling to everything we can and resist every downward step towards dependence. Dying people face so much anguish because they feel powerless, rejected, abandoned, and increasingly useless. Even Jesus, dying on a cross, suffered this anguish as he cried out, "My God, my God, why have you forsaken me?" (Matt. 27:46). I suspect at some level every dying person asks this question, and even if we are not dying the question is familiar to us. We know the emotion of feeling utterly abandoned and lost. Jesus moved from that moment of anguish to a state of surrender. Just before he died, he called out with a loud voice, "Father, into your hands I commit my spirit" (Lk. 23:46). Not all of us can make that final move to submission.

After his death and resurrection, Jesus told Peter, "Very truly I tell you, when you were younger you dressed yourself and went where you wanted; but when you are old you will stretch out your hands, and someone else will dress you and lead you where you do not want to go" (John 21:18). These words of Jesus describe a journey everyone facing a terminal illness knows all too well. The elderly also know this journey intimately. We will all face it, one way or another. As Dave's ALS progressed, he transitioned from independence to dependence. It began with weakness in his hands and a loss of dexterity in his fingers, so that he needed help to do up the buttons on his shirt (*and someone else will dress you*). Eventually he lost the ability to handle a spoon, knife, or fork (*and someone else will feed you*). And then he began to lose strength in his legs and was confined to a wheelchair (*and someone else will take you where you do not want to go*). Dave needed to be fed, bathed, clothed, and taken to the washroom. He became a little child again.

Many of us experience short episodes of this childlike dependence—times when we are very sick or injured and must rely on our loved ones to feed us, comfort us, and bring us pain medication. We rely on others to escort us to the bathroom or fetch a bedpan. Others prepare our meals and change our sheets. Every one of these experiences reminds us that we are children of God. Every period of dependence, long or short, foreshadows what our dying will be like. Every one is a gift from God moving us to a "divine dependence"[2] that will ultimately, if we are alert to it, prepare us for a good death.

You've likely participated in, or at least heard of, the team-building, trust-enhancing exercise where one member of the team stands with his back to the rest of the team, closes his eyes, relaxes, and simply falls backward. The rest of the team catches the one who falls so he does not hurt himself by crashing unprotected onto the floor. The faller needs to trust his catchers completely. The catchers need to do their jobs well. They demonstrate care and responsibility by how they catch. This is a simple little exercise used by management teams, youth groups, and self-help groups.

In dying, we don't trust human catchers, we trust the Catcher. In caring for the dying, we say repeatedly, "Don't be afraid. Remember, God loves you. He will catch you when you take your final fall. Let go and let Him catch you. He will be there. I know you can't see Him but He will be there. You will fall into Love."[3]

When our friend Helen first contracted cancer, she decided to live as normally as she could for as long as she could without bitterness or regret. When the cancer came back for the third time, Helen knew her days of normal independence were over. She died in peaceful dependence on God, who had guided her and loved her in life, confident he would guide her and love her in death. She also died in grateful dependence on loving friends and family. I remember the long list of caregivers who volunteered to sit with and serve Helen in her final days. Their presence allowed her to die at home, surrounded by love, treated with great respect. They gave Helen a precious gift, and Helen returned that gift to her friends as she allowed them to fulfill the deeply significant and satisfying role of caregivers. I don't know if Helen realized how much of a gift her dependent death was to her family and friends.

The family members of the dying also need to discover the gift of dependence. They, too, face great loss and an uncertain future. In many ways, their path may be harder because it only intensifies after death. When the sick one dies, their struggle ends, but the loss and grief have just begun for those left behind. The journey of the loved ones also moves from independence to dependence, from proving their strength to accepting the reality of their weakness, from frenetic do-gooding to peace-filled rest, from self-sufficiency to emptiness. It is one of the paradoxical promises of the kingdom that dependence on God leads to greater freedom. When we lose our life, we find it. When we take the yoke of Jesus upon us, we find rest. When we know our dependency lies in God and he holds us safely, we acknowledge there is no better place to be, no freer place, no more peaceful place, no more confident place, than in his arms, as a little child might rest in the arms of her mother or father.

THREE

Surrender

W HILE LUCIE WAS IN HER EARLY FORTIES, THE DOCTORS diagnosed her with an aggressive cancer that would ultimately take her life. Lucie could not get to that place of letting go and surrendering her life into God's care. She struggled greatly when she realized she was no longer in control and there was nothing else she, or anyone else, could do. I'm not sure she ever fully accepted the fact she was dying. I remember telling her what I thought was obvious—she had moved into the palliative stage of her care, and the doctors could do nothing beyond making her as comfortable as possible. I told her there were no more tests, no more treatments, no medical hope. And her response still startles me. Sitting in a wheelchair, so advanced in her cancer she had that all-too-familiar look of death—sunken cheeks, hollow eyes, pasty white skin—literally with days to live, she looked at me with confusion and fear and said, "I didn't know. How come no one told me?" The reality was she had been told many times in many ways but she simply could not accept her life was coming to an end and there was absolutely nothing she could do.

Surrender and dependency are interconnected. Sometimes they go together, but not always. Sometimes the dying grudgingly accept the loss of independence as their bodies fade away, but they never submit. They never surrender their lives, their futures, their dreams, their loved ones. Surrender is such a hard place to get to but absolutely worth the effort. If we allow it, death helps us engage and receive surrender as a life-giving gift.

Rather than giving up, surrender is letting go. It is overcoming the illusion we can control our situation, our environment, the medical system, or the universe. In surrender, we come to the conclusion that the universe unfolds without much help from you or me. We do not have to wake up early every morning to remind the sun to rise. We do not need to tell the tides whether they should come in or go out. The same power at work in the universe works in us, and yet we are often afraid to submit to that power.

Surrender comes with faith in God, who loves us and quite mysteriously loves the whole world in spite of the mess we have made. God desires that we live in the reality of his love and that we surrender into that love, knowing he will not abandon us, even in death. In letting go, we release our idea of how things should turn out and accept what is happening to us. We actually do not know what would be best for us. In looking back on their lives, the dying begin to see that bad situations sometimes led them to better places, and that what appeared good at the time didn't turn out all that well. During the times we thought we absolutely knew what was best, we were likely wrestling with illusions. Surrender is letting go of knowing where life will take us.

Whether in times of war or police activity, or, for most of us, in the pretend world of movies and TV, we have all seen and heard the command "Hands up!" Two arms raised in the air symbolize surrender. Often, refusing to surrender can have severe consequences. Surrender accepts what cannot be changed. Perhaps there are more of them than of you, or they are stronger, or they have bigger guns. Whatever the circumstances, you have no choice but to surrender. There is wisdom in the act of surrender. Wisdom and hope. You are still alive and may yet be rescued.

But better than *hands up* is the image of *palms up*—a free-will, intentional decision to turn our palms upward and declare to God, "I am ready to accept whatever you have for me, whether I understand it or not. I don't give up wanting to live. I don't give up on treatment options or doing whatever I can to increase my chances of survival. I place my life in your loving hands, knowing you see things and know things I do not see and cannot know. I surrender into your love."

Lucie never got to that place of a *palms-up* surrender. She challenged everything. Lucie tried to control her life and manage her treatments and care long beyond her ability to do so in any constructive way. She could not let go. She did not go gently into the night. She did not fall back and let the God of the universe catch her. She fought.

There is something heroic about Lucie, something we admire, something that appeals to our culture: *We will never surrender! Never say die!* Lucie approached her disease the way she approached much of life—a problem to solve, an obstacle to work through, a crisis to conquer. She believed if you were smart enough and if you worked hard enough and got access to the necessary resources, you could overcome anything. Much of the business world operates this way. We reward and admire such people. Death comes as a paradigm-shifting shock to these people, because no amount of wisdom or resources will help. You just cannot beat death.

Many of the dying discover the control they thought they had was never real. We typically do not understand this until we find ourselves in the middle of some crisis and our well-ordered lives begin to crack and crumble. We also tend to equate control with freedom. As long as we maintain control, we assume we are free to live the way we want for as long as we want. But this is simply not true. The dying realize freedom is found in surrender.

Liz Dunn, the troubled, central character in Douglas Coupland's novel *Eleanor Rigby*, puts it this way: "I decided that instead of demanding certainty from life, I now wanted peace. No more trying to control everything—it was now time to go with the flow. With that one decision, the chain-mail shroud I'd been wearing my entire life fell from my body and I was light as a gull. I'd freed myself."[4]

Sometimes, family members and friends struggle with surrender as they attempt to control the disease, the medical system, God, and even the person who is sick. I greatly respect anyone who gives generously and sacrificially of their time, energy, and money to provide every possibility of healing for their loved one. They would move heaven and earth to find a cure or to stop the pain. However, sometimes their well-intended actions cross the line from loving support to a control that inflicts more harm than good. This can result in conflict between the dying and those who love them.

Lorie very aggressively managed the treatments and care for her husband, Dave, throughout his three-year struggle with ALS. She always looked for alternative treatments, and when she discovered something new, she pleaded with Dave to give it a try. Lorie worked tirelessly to find a cure or, at least, some relief from the downward spiral of this horrible, wasting disease. Two years after Dave passed away, I invited Lorie to participate with me in a teaching series on death and dying. Here is part of what she shared:

> I'm the kind of person that likes to be in control. I figured that if I researched enough, did enough, loved him enough, had enough prayer rallies and brought him to enough doctors, Dave would be healed. At one point we were going to three naturopaths at the same

time. Dave went to please me, but all the time he kept saying, "Honey, let God be God." Surrendering people I love to God has not been an easy thing for me. But I've learned that I'm not the one in control, God is.

When loving caregivers find the courage to surrender, they offer a profound gift to the dying—they stop the frenetic activity, they stop trying to control what cannot be controlled—they let God be God.

Often the last and most excruciating act of surrender for those who are dying is to surrender their loved ones. Even those who are completely at peace with their own death find it almost impossible to abandon their loved ones. "Who will take care of them?" "Who will help them?" "How will they get along without me?" "I don't want them to be sad when I die." That was Vicky's worry for her daughters and grandchild. That was Lucie's worry for her children. That was Helen's worry for her husband, Roy. That was Dave's worry for his family. In these times I would remind them, in the same way God would be faithful in death, he would remain faithful in life. And, together, we would contemplate the hard-to-grasp truth that God loves our family members more than we do. He is more invested in them than we are and he has way more ability to look after them than we do.

I am grateful that most of the people with whom I journeyed in their season of dying discovered the peace and comfort of a courageous surrender. They stopped the fighting, the worrying, the fearing, and entered into a place of trust, contentment, and peace. All still hoped for a cure, but eventually acknowledged it was out of their hands and made peace with that knowledge. Trusting in God and others to care for them and not to abandon them, they believed in an ultimate good outcome: death is a doorway to eternity with God. They surrendered into love.

Surrender is not just for the dying. Every day, every moment, and every situation provides an opportunity for us to learn from those who are dying the wisdom and freedom of letting go. We have no choice but to trust in a force bigger than ourselves in our birth and again in our death. But between life and death we get lost because we forget to surrender.

A number of years ago, Mo came into my office. Mo had been our lead Youth Pastor for about five years, but I had a pretty good idea things were about to change. Mo had shared with me in recent months about his inner turmoil. He and God had been wrestling about his future, about playing it safe, about total submission. He told me his time in our well-to-do community was coming to an end, and God was calling him and his family to serve the poor of Africa. As Mo shared, it became clear God had moved him and his wife to a complete state of submission. I vividly remember the tenderness and the brokenness in Mo as he explained he finally reached that place in his heart where he let it all go and said to God: "I will do anything. I will go anywhere. I will go any time." That's surrender. Mo and his family now live in Malawi loving the orphans and the widows, the hungry and the diseased. God is doing incredible things in them and through them. When you surrender to God, the adventure really begins.

I hesitate to include this story because it supports one of our stereotypical fears. If we really surrender to God, he will ask us to go to Africa. And he might. But more likely, your adventure with God will take place within the city or town where you currently live. But where you end up is all part of surrendering. Anything. Anywhere. Anytime.

As I write this, I am reminded of the terribly difficult and highly suspect position God put Mary in when he chose to send Jesus to earth through Mary's womb. Luke tells us Mary was greatly troubled, and with good reason. She was inexplicably pregnant, and not by her fiancé. What kind of future could she hope for? Mary listened to the angel explain what God was up to and what her part would be in God's great plan (Luke 1:26-38). Mary's brilliant response is simple, profound and courageous. She says, "I am the Lord's servant. May it be to me just as you have said" (38, CEB). What an incredible act of surrender and faith. Richard Neuhaus says "Let it be" is Mary's great fiat. It is not fatalism, but faith. Fatalism is resigning ourselves to the inevitable. Faith is entrusting ourselves to the One who is eternally trustworthy, who is worthy of trust.[5]

FOUR

Community

I FIRST MET IRIS, A MIDDLE-AGED SINGLE WOMAN, when she began attending our church. Iris joined our small group, and before long we became friends. A little while later, I hired Iris to manage our church's new non-profit housing complex. Iris's no-nonsense approach to life suited the role. She was a survivor—tough childhood, divorced, no family close by. But God's Spirit softened her over the years, and she developed a real affection for the poor of our community. I first believed God brought her to us at just the right time for the express purpose of running our housing ministry. But I was wrong. God brought her to us so she could die. Two years into her job, Iris began complaining of fatigue and unusual physical pains. The doctors quickly discovered an advanced and aggressive cancer. Iris quit work and devoted all of her remaining energy to enduring chemotherapy treatments. But there would be no remission for Iris—she was dying.

In a move that took Iris (and me) quite by surprise, Roy and Helen, a couple in our congregation, decided she should not spend her final days in a hospital and offered to let her die in their home. For the couple, their gracious and loving act not only was a gift to Iris but also ended up being preparation for the journey Helen herself would later endure.

Iris was overwhelmed at the offer and was shocked that people cared for her so much. Since she had no family of her own, our church had become her family. With the help of doctors and nurses from our church and with the help of a palliative care team from the local hospital, Iris spent her final weeks surrounded by loving friends and caregivers in the warm environment of a home rather than in a clinical and sterile hospital ward. Iris died with grace and dignity. Iris died in community.

A number of years after Iris's death, Helen discovered she had ovarian cancer. As Helen neared the end of her five-year battle with the disease, we all knew where she would die. She, too, spent her final days in her home, in the same room occupied by Iris years before, surrounded by family, friends, and caregivers. I remember the round-the-clock roster of volunteers who signed up to spend precious time with Helen. They considered it an honor and a privilege. I remember the equipment and supplies being brought into the home to care for Helen. I remember the sense of community that pervaded the home in those weeks. The oven never lacked for food and the kitchen table always boasted a pot of tea and a plate of cookies. Three or four and often more people attended to Helen and Roy at all times—loving them, being the community of Christ to them.

When the family, church, neighbors, caregivers, and friends gathered at Helen's home, they came not just to say their good-byes but also to encourage, support, and help in any way they could: prayers and hugs, muffins and meals, running errands, looking after the house—anything at all to make life a little more bearable. Mostly, they came to cry and to remember, to witness the final passage of a woman they loved, a woman of God. The gift of their presence, let alone all the practical acts of support, reminded Roy and Helen they were loved.

Helen died not only as a beloved daughter of God, but as a beloved wife and mother, a beloved family member and friend. She lived and died in community. In some strange but very real way, Helen's dying called the community into existence. I am not suggesting that community exists only when someone dies, but community often springs to life in the midst of death and dying. Community becomes a sweet aroma both to the dying and to those left behind that counters in some small way the bitter stench of loss. It cannot replace the loss, but somehow it makes the loss bearable. Whenever the community of care gathers, they address the fear of rejection and abandonment held by the sick and dying because they consider themselves a burden or nuisance. These fears have been heightened in recent years as our culture works hard at hiding and sanitizing death. For decades now, the civilized West has been on a march to remove from public view the ugly, dirty, and upsetting aspects of life. While violent death on TV and in the movies (the safe kind of spectator death that objectifies the experience and does not demand our personal involvement) runs at an all-time high, real death, the kind of close-up and personal death that threatens to unnerve us, has gone into hiding. The French social historian Philippe Aries calls this modern phenomenon the "Invisible Death."

> The hidden death in the hospital began very discreetly in the 1930s and 1940s and became widespread after 1950. . . . Our senses can no longer tolerate the sights and smells that in the early nineteenth century were part of daily life, along with suffering and illness. The physiological effects have passed from daily life to the aseptic world of hygiene, medicine and morality. The perfect manifestation of this world is the hospital, with its cellular discipline. . . . Although it is not always admitted, the hospital has offered families a place where they can hide the unseemly invalid whom neither the world nor they can endure. . . . The hospital has become the place of solitary death.[6]

Many of the dying spend their final days in the intensive care ward or the critical care unit. By being isolated among strangers, their fear of being abandoned in the last hours comes true—they are abandoned to the good intentions of highly skilled professionals who barely know them.[7]

Fortunately, in recent years, society has pushed back against these invisible deaths. More and more of the dying and their caregivers choose to spend the final weeks of life in homes or in hospices. And most hospitals now provide much more compassionate palliative care wards in support of the dying and their community of care. All of this seeks to restore the hope that "our last moments will be guided not by the bioengineers but by those who know who we are."[8]

John, a young, artistic, gifted man, faced numerous health challenges that dated back to his childhood. John spent many years fully participating in the life of our church family before a brain tumor began to slowly but surely erode his well-being. After a multi-year battle with the cancer, John and his family made the decision to spend their final days in a local hospice. This beautiful home now serves as a six-bedroom care facility for the dying. Each room is tastefully decorated with comfortable chairs, dressers, night stands, lamps, pictures on the wall, and big bright windows overlooking spacious gardens, grass, and trees. In this setting, family and friends, some of whom had come from great distances, surrounded John with their presence, their love, and their care. I remember the respect and dignity given to John by the hospice staff, many of them volunteers. The hospice felt like a home and had, in fact, become home for John, his family, and his friends.

The community of care is a real community, caring not only for the dying person but for one another as they bear one another's grief, comfort one another, laugh and cry together, remember together, eat and pass time together. In all this, they share a common bond of suffering and find comfort in being together, showing up even when it is not their allotted shift.

The community of care fulfills a divine purpose, reminding the dying they are still loved. They have not been forgotten or abandoned or rejected but remain valued and cherished, not only by God but by us. The community of care, by its very presence, challenges the many lies that the dying face: they are useless; they no longer serve any purpose; no one wants to be around them anymore; they are a burden. The community provides a divine, profound, life-giving gift to the dying.

Henri Nouwen wisely warns that "caring for the dying is not for the faint of heart and it is not to be done alone."[9] Death's dark power needs respect. Watching a loved one die can cause anguished sorrow and overwhelming feelings of helplessness. At times we secretly wish it would all end soon, and then we are plagued with guilt for wishing them dead. If at all possible, care for the dying should happen in community.

I have, over the last decade, been witness to much dying. And part of my calling, part of my role as a pastor and caregiver is, at times, to bear the grief of others. Sometimes we need others to bear our sorrows. Family members and friends share a collective grief as a loved one passes that none could bear alone, but when shared it becomes possible, though just barely. To the well-known African proverb, "It takes a village to raise a child," we could safely add, "It takes a community to care for the dying."

FIVE

Communion

Andrew's funeral was unique in so many ways. Whenever I preside over or participate in a funeral service, I always wear my funeral suit—standard issue, black, conservative, dignified. Andrew's funeral was the first, and continues to be the only, funeral to which I did not wear my funeral suit. At Andrew's request, we wore bright, colorful, casual clothes because this was to be a celebration. Andrew also requested balloons instead of flowers. He wanted a party. Andrew's funeral was also exceptional by its length—it went nearly three hours. What was even more remarkable is no one seemed to care. There was, however, a rush to the washrooms as soon as the service concluded. More than the clothes, balloons, and length, this particular service was marked by the sense of what I can only describe as communion—a feeling of oneness, intimacy, wonder, and awe.

Andrew lived to be one of the oldest survivors of childhood brain cancer in Canada. At the age of 10, Andrew began his journey of surgeries and treatments for an aggressive brain tumor. He was never the same—never able to walk and run and jump like the other kids, and he talked a little funny. He was an incredibly captivating character who loved conversation and shared his opinions even if you didn't ask. In spite of the deficits caused by the cancer and subsequent treatments, Andrew lived abundantly. After graduation from college, Andrew became an entrepreneur, first starting a doll house enterprise which was then followed by a backyard playground business.

He later founded Rebounders Canada, an organization for the adult survivors of childhood cancer, with the motto "Thriving not just Surviving." Rebounders grew nationally, allowing a large network of survivors to connect, build friendships, and find a safe community that gives meaning and purpose to their lives. Andrew was a member of the Junior Board of Trade and of Rotary. He received two local awards for his services to the community. Perhaps his two greatest achievements, however, were getting married to an incredible fellow survivor, Jill, and against all odds becoming the father of two healthy boys.

Andrew lived knowing he would die sooner than most of us. His numerous doctor appointments, hospital visits, and physical challenges were a constant reminder he was different—that each day was a gift not to be wasted. To say Andrew was unique is both absolutely true and totally inadequate. I do not expect to see anyone quite as courageous and stubborn and compassionate and filled with life as Andrew again in my lifetime.

Andrew's faith in the all-loving and all-powerful God was quite remarkable. Given his circumstances, we might well understand if Andrew strongly questioned God's love and doubted God's power. I could easily have understood a little skepticism, a little bitterness, a little distance, but there was none of that. Andrew took great comfort in the knowledge that God was God, and he never doubted God's love; he trusted in God's provision like few people I have ever known. Andrew always had big plans far beyond his capacity to make them happen, and after telling me of his plans, he always concluded, "God will do it. I don't know how, but God will do it."

There are some people in this world who have the special gift of making us better just because of who they are. Andrew was that kind of person. Encounters with Andrew always left me in a better state—more encouraged, inspired, humbled, redirected, grounded, reflective, more spiritually attuned—just better.

The week before Andrew died, he was able to attend and participate in an anniversary party celebrating 15 years of marriage to his loving wife, Jill. Towards the end of the celebration, Andrew began saying his good-byes, predicting he would die within the next few days. True to his word, he died three days later. Andrew spent his life giving other people hope. Andrew endured pain with a smile to the end, and on the day before he died he went on his motorized tricycle, in excruciating pain, to buy bottled water for a group of parched workmen assembling a children's play center in his local park. They were so surprised at his gift, as were Andrew's friends and family.

I share some of Andrew's story to set the stage for his Celebration of Life service. As I mentioned, it was quite unlike anything I have experienced. One of the things that struck me even before I stood up to welcome everyone was the buzz in the air. This was not a somber event. The room was filled with conversation, movement, people greeting and hugging one another, and an unusual amount of laughter. I also realized that within the packed church were many distinct groups. Andrew and Jill's families were there, to be sure, but so was the church family and also the Rebounder family and members of the local business community and friends and neighbors—all drawn together by the man now dead, Andrew. As the afternoon proceeded, these disparate communities grew to appreciate one another. We enjoyed hearing about Andrew from different perspectives. We clapped, cheered, cried, and laughed as complete strangers shared about Andrew's compelling and fascinating life.

And no matter what tribe we identified with, we all waited, most somewhat nervously and some expectantly, for a portion in

the program where it was clearly written "Jill Sprawson (Dance)."
Andrew's wife, Jill, was going to dance at her husband's funeral! Jill,
herself a childhood cancer survivor, was not a typical dancer. She
had no training and wasn't endowed with the physical gracefulness
one might associate with a dancer. I know there were many who
expected this might be somewhat charming, at best, or a disaster, at
worst. Just as Jill introduced her dance and explained she would be
dancing in worship of God and in memory of Andrew, I glanced
over to her children and saw one of the boys had his head in his
hands, unable to watch what his mother was about to do. We all
held our breath.

What Jill lacked in grace and form, she more than made up
for in pure joy. Jill's dance morphed into a beautiful expression
of emotion and movement and worship and celebration. It
was stunning, and we could not look away—we were drawn in,
mesmerized by her complete lack of self-consciousness, her
abandon and freedom. As she concluded, we all burst into loud
applause with many in tears. Through her dance, Jill connected
us, creating a unique communion amongst the hundreds of people
who had gathered to honor a man they dearly loved. Andrew's
death brought us into the same room, and Jill's dance brought us
into spiritual and emotional communion.

Communion is more personal, more intimate and more mysterious than community. Communion suggests a oneness and a union
that often refers to an intimate connection between God and his
followers. It also refers to a deep sharing of thoughts and emotions
among people. The notion of communion carries with it a sense of
the sacred. In communion, we find a dimension that goes beyond
normal conversation and human emotion. Something else is at work.
Although I do not fully understand it, communion is one of death's
most significant gifts.

Do you remember the weeks following the collapse of the World Trade Center towers in New York City on September 11, 2001? What eventually became known as *ground zero* became sacred territory—a place of communion. People would gather there by the hundreds and by the thousands to reflect, to mourn, to pray. Death brought them together—they did not want to be alone. The death of Princess Diana in 1997 evoked a national response in England the likes of which most of us had never seen. The gates of Kensington Palace became sacred space—a place of profound mourning, a place of oneness, a place of union in the midst of national grief. Strangers were brought together by a single death. And in Canada, we have the Highway of Heroes. Every time a Canadian soldier dies in active duty, his or her body is flown to a military base in Trenton, Ontario, for a repatriation ceremony. Military policy dictates each soldier's body must be examined by a coroner in Toronto. For this journey, a hearse carrying the body of the fallen soldier travels the stretch of Highway 401 from Trenton to Toronto. A small convoy of police, military vehicles, and limousines for family members accompanies the hearse. Without any formal organization, Canadian citizens— men, women, and children—gather along the route by the hundreds, often positioning themselves on overpasses along the route, silently honoring and saluting one of their own. As they gather and wait and honor, they enter into communion. And the same thing happens at every funeral, every memorial service, every celebration of one who has passed away. Death unites us. Communion comes as a gift in the midst of death.

Most of our lives, we are coached and encouraged to be different, to stand apart from the crowd. And this kind of distinction brings a certain joy and exhilaration. The Bible encourages us to do everything with excellence. We like the message of independence and excellence. We like to think we might be different and perhaps even better than others.

Death, however, teaches me a message equally exciting and even more profound. At the core of our being, we are just like everyone else. We are all born powerless and we all die powerless, and our little differences in life dwindle in the light of this enormous truth.[10] In fact, as we think deeply upon our death, the things that separate us here on earth, things such as money, power, status, appearance, and intelligence, diminish in significance. If we allow, death draws us into greater solidarity, not only with our loved ones, but with all of humanity.

When I visited Mongolia, a country still struggling to recover from the collapse of the Soviet Union, I was struck by the poverty of the nomadic herdsmen—not the starvation kind of poverty, just the absolute basic-necessities-of-life kind of poverty. We ate congee (boiled rice) each day for breakfast and endured a fatty, gristly mutton soup for lunch and dinner. Our hosts did not have much, but what they had, they shared with us. During my travels to India, I experienced a much harsher poverty—the starvation, dying-on-the-streets kind of poverty. I realize now I have much in common with the nomads of Mongolia and the beggars of India. They will almost certainly die in poverty. But so will I. We all die poor. In the final days of our life, nothing can keep us from dying. Whatever accumulated wealth, whatever power or status we have obtained, whatever access to medical experts we might have, no matter who we know and no matter how much knowledge we have attained, nothing can keep us from dying. Nouwen calls this "true poverty."[11] The men, women, and children of Mongolia and India are my brothers and sisters.

When Jesus hung on the cross, he engaged in a brief, life-changing conversation with a common criminal, also hanging on a cross. Rome had crucified both Jesus and the criminal for their alleged crimes. Their conversation underscores our equality in death. The criminal asks Jesus to remember him, and Jesus acknowledges they will both die that very day but also assures the man they will both enter paradise together. What strikes me as utterly profound is death brought the God-man, Jesus, and the earth-man criminal to the same place—the end of their physical lives. From a human perspective, death completely unified Jesus and the criminal. If that is true of Jesus and the criminal, how much more is it true of every man, woman, and child who has ever lived and died? A deep and profound union takes place in our death. We die in solidarity with the rest of humankind. We are truly brothers and sisters. If we could only somehow take hold of this reality while we are still healthy! Can you imagine how the world might change?

SIX

Remember

A COUPLE OF YEARS AGO, JAMES AND I MET FOR BREAKFAST at the local Golden Griddle. We talked about family and sports and work and the future. Then he asked about my book, and this started a conversation about my death and dying experiences. In the middle of this conversation, James started talking about his cousin Sammy. James hardly got two sentences out before he choked up. He looked away, composed himself, and said, "This happens every time I try to talk about my cousin—there's something inside of me that is somehow connected to Sammy." James was just 13 years old when Sammy died, and every time he thinks of his cousin something wells up inside that he cannot explain or control. I asked James if he had ever told the story of Sammy to anyone. He said he hadn't. I suggested he might want to write about Sammy's life and death. The next day, James sent me a beautiful gift—his story about his cousin. It resonated deeply within me, reducing me to tears and to laughter in equal measure. In addition to the story of his cousin, James also wrote about his experience of telling the story.

It has become clear to me that a cousin who passed away when I was a teenager is buried somewhere in me. I am not sure why. But, there is a place that my cousin occupies in my soul that I am unable to explain . . . whenever I think about him, I cry. And, I don't cry much. Well, that is not true. I cry at joyful things. I cry when I am proud of my kids. I cry when I am part of something beautiful. I cry when I see the human spirit prevail. I cry in church. But, I don't cry when I am sad. Except when I think of Sammy.

Here I sit at a kitchen table with tears in my eyes. I am 50 years old. I think about Sammy rarely, but every time I do, I just cry. Why do I cry? Did I never get to cry then? I can't remember.

Is it the loss of innocence? Was that the point in time I realized life was not perfect? That bad things happen to good people? Did something in Sammy's death reveal how vulnerable I am? All I know is that there was a lid sealed over the pain I felt about his passing at the same time they put one on his coffin. And, it is still in there.

Where does Sammy fit in my life? Why is it that I have such an emotional reaction to talking about him? It has been 37 years! But, he is still alive in my soul. It is a reminder that we all have an influence on each other. My formative years were punctuated by his passing. It created a hole that could not be filled in, as much as I tried.

He was so loved. He still is.

The pain is a manifestation of something real, not imagined. It is about losing someone suddenly, who was an element of my being. He probably had no idea how much he meant to me and I never got to tell him. My life has been lived with him inside me. He is meant to be there. He is a reminder. We are all weak. None of us can live in isolation. None of us can be without pain. None of us can avoid it. No shell can hold it. We are human. That is both our blessing and our curse.

Oh God, I would like to see him again someday. I
hope he sees me. I hope he is proud. I hope he is well.

Many of us have our "Sammy's"—stories of death and dying
locked away in our hearts and in our history. It is so important
to remember and tell their stories. Keeping them hidden only
ensures new life will not emerge. Being willing to face the pain,
confusion, and loss brought about by death brings the very real
possibility something beautiful can yet emerge—that new life will
come. Although death remains a source of deep pain, it can also
be carefully and reverently mined as a source of healing. I do not
know where James's courageous journey into his cousin's death
will take him, but it is already a gift to him, to his family, to me,
and to anybody who reads about Sammy. I experienced many
emotions while reading about Sammy. One of them was a sense of
joy for my friend. He opened the door and looked at death, and
out flowed a beautiful, bittersweet story of love and life and loss.

Jesus emphasized the importance of remembering when he
celebrated the Passover feast with his disciples. In an act of preparation
for his death, Jesus shared bread and wine with his friends. As Jesus
told them plainly he would soon die, he created communion with his
closest companions—a union of emotions, anxieties, feelings, fears,
and expectations. In this highly symbolic act, Jesus took common
bread and blessed and broke it, literally tore it apart, and gave it to
them. And he said, "This is what my body will be like. Whenever
you eat this bread, think of me not in despair but in hope of what
my death will accomplish." And he took some common wine and he
poured it into a cup and blessed it, and as he passed it to his dearest
friends he said, "This cup is the new covenant in my blood which
will be poured out for you. Whenever you drink the cup remember

me, not in sadness, but in anticipation of a new day, a new world, a new covenant, that will result from my death."

We have in these acts and in these words of Jesus the basis of our call to regularly remember Jesus. He said it twice. We need to take this more literally. We need to tell stories about Jesus. We should remind each other about what Jesus did and said. We might laugh or cry as we tell each other about the reality of Jesus in our lives or why at times he feels so distant. We remember by telling stories and being truthful, by honoring the memory of the One who died for us. We celebrate his goodness, his kindness, his love. We reflect on the reality that our lives are better because of his death.

We lift up Jesus as our model for life, and there is none better. But I wonder if we should pay more attention to Jesus as the model for our death. What if those of us who are dying said to our loved ones and our friends, "When I am no longer here, keep remembering me when you come together to eat, drink, and celebrate."

When we gather for a family meal, whether on a regular weekday evening or a special occasion such as a birthday or Christmas, we should not shy away from raising a glass in fond memory of our friends and loved ones who have died. We should *remember*. Tell stories. Laugh. Cry. Be silent. As we do, we share in a communion that transcends death.

Jesus claimed—no, he *promised*—his death would be good for us, would make our lives better, richer, more meaningful. God intends our deaths to be good for others as well. If we live well and die well, we will leave a lasting and positive influence on those who follow. A good death points us in the right direction. As painful as the loss may be, we are better because of the death. Good deaths do not happen all the time nor do they take away the pain and mess and grief. But, they bring new life. Reflecting on how the life and death of a loved one has made our world better can bring healing and hope to our soul.

SEVEN

Reverence

A STRONG AND PERSISTENT VOICE INSIDE MY HEAD warns me not to talk about the death of children. Little in this world disturbs me more. I cannot make any sense of it. I do not like what goes on inside my heart when a child dies. The world closes in and everything grows dark. Something begins to crack inside, and I feel like I'm going to break. I feel that the world *has* broken. I do not know what to do. I do not know how to think. And I feel way too much.

Sad is such a feeble word in these circumstances. *Tragic* does not begin to convey the emotional devastation. The death of a child is way beyond sad, way beyond tragic—it feels so utterly wrong.

Early on in my pastoral ministry at Chartwell Baptist Church, I encountered the unthinkable: a young couple's little girl had drowned at a family cottage. And they came to me for help. Although this was over 20 years ago, I still vividly remember my first meeting with the grief-stricken mom and dad. As they entered my office, everything about them—their faces, the slump of their shoulders, the way they walked, their eyes—spoke of overwhelming grief. With their torn-apart lives and their broken hearts, they no longer seemed completely human. I remember fighting to hold myself together as I listened to their story. I was at a total loss. How does one speak love and comfort and peace and hope into such a senseless and useless event? What do you say to parents who have lost their little child? Do you tell them God must have had a reason? Do you tell them this will make them grow stronger? Do you tell them it's all part of God's divine plan? Do you tell them their little girl has been saved from a lifetime of living in an evil and harsh world? Do you tell them it's going to be okay? Do you tell them time heals everything? Please tell me! What do you say?

How could I bring peace and comfort and healing to this couple when I could barely contain my own emotions? We had two little girls about the same age. I could not imagine how we would cope had that been us. On the drive home after that first meeting, my tears began to tumble out. I stopped the car because I could not see the road. My heart ached for them. I was afraid for my little girls. Mainly, I was afraid for me—not afraid of my death but afraid of what might happen to me if death came for my girls. Death is powerful and absolutely final. There is no negotiating. I was not sure I would survive.

As is the case of many couples faced with the loss of a child, this couple's marriage did not make it. All kinds of relational issues surfaced, and they moved into blaming, bitter sorrow and, ultimately, separation. In the end, the pain of their loss proved too much. It does not have to be this way.

Bob and Leslie are two of our dearest friends. In many ways, they have been models for life and faith. Bob and Leslie survived the death of not one but two children, their only children. Their deaths, coming in rapid succession, moved me from a state of barely coping to not coping at all. Were it not for Bob and Leslie's unbelievably gracious, humble, and reverent response to the death of their children, I fear I might have drowned in a sea of grief, confusion, and despair.

On April 7, 2004, Bob came into my office, and I knew immediately something was wrong. Bob told me his daughter, Karen, 40 years old, had just been diagnosed with advanced cancer. And for the first time in my nearly 10 years of knowing Bob, he began to cry. Many tears have been shed since. Physically and medically, the next 14 months were devastating for the Bernardo family, as Karen pursued a variety of treatment options to no avail. We prayed for healing; we hoped for a miracle. The medical system had no answers, and God seemed reluctant to act. The last few months, in particular, were challenging as Karen's body began to shut down from the effects of the cancer. With Karen's permission, Bob and Leslie decided Karen would be cared for in their home. Leslie became her primary caregiver and Bob her primary encourager. Every morning, before heading off to work, Bob would hand-write a note to Karen and stick it under her door. These notes were filled with reminders of God's enduring love for each one of them and of a father's enduring love for his only daughter.

It was such a privilege to spend time with Karen, listening to her questions and having deep conversations about the promises of God, the frailties of human relationships, the disappointments of life, and the timeless truths of God. Karen's belief and faith in God who loved her, in Jesus who died for her, in the Heavenly Father who had already secured a place for her in eternity never wavered. She had strong, bold faith. But she had questions, and we would talk for hours about her questions. And when her questions got too hard or complex or deep, I would have to shrug and tell her, "I don't know, Karen." And Karen would say, "I know you don't know. I don't think anyone knows."

Karen's greatest concern as she thought about her death was for her parents. Karen correctly understood her death would cause untold heartache to her mother and father. It was the wrong order of operations—grandparents first, then parents, never children first. And for a season, she took comfort in the knowledge her older brother, Geoff, would look after them, should the Lord not heal her.

Without warning, six weeks before Karen breathed her last, Geoff suffered a serious stroke. He lived with his wife, Vita, and their little daughter, Phoebe. Vita found him lying on the floor of his study on a Monday morning and called 911. Late on Wednesday night, Bob and Leslie received a call from the hospital that Geoff's condition had worsened and he was not expected to last the night. Bob called me at 11 PM, and together we drove to Peterborough, leaving Leslie and Karen to comfort one another at home. By the time we arrived, it was already too late—Geoff was gone. Vita was at his side and various machines were keeping his body alive, but his brain had stopped functioning. It was a long night and an even longer next day. No one slept.

Throughout the night and throughout the next day, as we spent many hours together, I often looked into the sad eyes of my dear friend Bob and knew I had no answers. No profound insights. Nothing to make the pain go away. All I could do was be there and make sure he was not alone—cry with him, pray with him, give him a hug, help him talk things through. That seemed like so little, but maybe it was enough.

All by itself, Geoff's sudden death was tragic and devastating, but put in the context of Karen's life and death struggle, it defied comprehension. Karen attended her brother's funeral in a wheelchair, staying at the back of the church in case she might need medical attention. Karen was almost dead. Her brother was completely dead.

Forty-four days later, we assembled in the same church to honor and celebrate Karen's life, and then we went to the same cemetery and laid her body in a grave right beside that of her brother.

In the end, Vita and Phoebe were left without a husband and father, and Bob and Leslie were left without their children. It seemed like a cruel joke. More than once, I wondered silently and out loud, had the Lord misjudged? Wasn't this too much for one family to bear? What is going on here, God? What are you doing? What were you thinking? It seemed evil had won the day.

These were some of the most confusing and profoundly sad months of my life. Strangely, being with Bob and Leslie during this time and the honor of presiding over the celebration services of their children proved to be deeply spiritual. I wanted to be no other place than walking with my friends in the painful journey of their loss.

It is hard to adequately describe how Bob and Leslie reacted and responded to loss and grief most of us cannot even comprehend. I have tried. I've tried to think about what it would be like to lose our two girls and I cannot. My mind will not go there. And so, it has been hard to process Bob and Leslie's ability to navigate their devastating loss. To say it was remarkable, inspiring, dumbfounding, would be inadequate.

In their season of death, Bob and Leslie lived what they lived in every other season of their lives. They were entirely consistent with who I knew them to be before their children got sick and died. They had a deep and rich faith before and after. They believed in God's sovereignty before and after. They experienced God's love before and after. Bob spoke at both funerals—spoke of gratitude for the years God had given them as a family, spoke of unshakable faith in a God who held the keys of life and death, and spoke of mystery. It was Bob's way of worshiping God in the midst of unthinkable loss. What a profound and illogical response to grief.

It's not that Bob did not grieve or experience deeply the sense of loss. Years after Geoff and Karen passed away, Bob surprised himself by winning a golf tournament at his home course. Having played with Bob frequently, I, too, was surprised when he called to share his good news. We sent him a congratulatory card. A few weeks later, as we were talking about his win, he told me how much he wished he could have called Geoff and Karen. He never felt his loss more keenly than when he had good news to share. He said he thought about his children every day of his life. His heart missed them terribly even while his mind was settled, knowing God was sovereign and loving and good. He and Leslie never wavered in their conviction that they would see their children again with God.

It is hard not to think of the Old Testament story of Job in these circumstances. Bob and Leslie, like Job, were upright and righteous. Bob and Leslie were two of the most gracious, God-honoring, spiritually mature people I have ever known. Two finer people would be hard to find. Like Job, they suffered enormous and inexplicable loss. Bob and Leslie were blessed with two healthy, bright, thoughtful, smart children, and within the span of 44 days, both were dead.

When tragic events unfold here on earth and there seems to be no explanation, the story of Job reminds us there is another world of which we know precious little. Job's story plays out on two stages. There is the lower stage of earth where Job and his friends discuss the tragic events that have transpired in Job's life, and there is the upper stage of the heavenlies—the spiritual realm where God and his angels and Satan and his demons exist. The upper stage is the other world. And what strikes me so powerfully about this story is that in this world—with our emotions of sadness and grief and loss as well as joy and new life and great purpose— there is so much we do not know and cannot see. Job and his friends were unaware of what was taking place in the heavenlies. That gives me some comfort.

There is so much more going on here than the passing of two young lives into eternity. Geoff's story and Karen's story are not finished yet—there is more to come. The impact of their lives does not end with their death. God's plan to redeem the world does not falter because Geoff suffered a stroke and Karen contracted cancer. His plan continues, and somehow, mysteriously, God's plan includes death. I do not understand this. Please don't ask me to explain it. I do not know what God has in store for Vita and Phoebe, Bob and Leslie, relatives and friends, but this story is not over. And I suspect there is new life yet to emerge out of these deaths.

After a series of strange and inexplicable tragedies, Job and his friends spend days discussing, complaining, accusing, ranting, confronting, crying, and shouting. The friends basically blame Job for what has happened and Job basically blames God. God finally speaks and says, "You don't know what you're talking about. You have no idea what's going on." This is a sobering reminder God is God and we are not.

Who are we to try to make sense out of things that do not make sense? Who are we to declare what God should have done or ought not to have done? Who are we to try to take these mind-numbing events and reduce them to simplistic religious truisms? And so I resist the temptation to tell Vita that Geoff is in a better place. We know that's true, but it does not help Vita and Phoebe and does not explain why Geoff had to die at such a young age. I resist the temptation to tell Bob and Leslie that God's purposes all work out for good for those that serve the Lord. As followers of Jesus, we affirm God is working out his plans to redeem the world, but that does not help Bob and Leslie understand how that plan could possibly have included the taking of their son and daughter. And so I come back to my belief there is more going on here than we can see. We do not know the full story, and that gives me hope. The story does not end with a grave.

God's response to Job and his friends does not answer the question of "why" but it does answer the question of "who." God says to Job, "Who are you that you question me without knowledge? Who are you that you try to correct the Almighty? Who are you to accuse me that I don't know what I'm doing?" And in one of the most dramatic declarations of God's sovereignty and power and knowledge, God begins to ask Job all kinds of impossible questions:

> Do you know where lightning comes from?
> Can you direct the path of the storm?
> Do you send the lightning bolts on their way?
> Do you know where the snow is stored, or where the hail
>   originates?
> Are you there when the doe bears her fawn?
> Did you teach the hawk to fly?
> —Job 38, 39

God knows the impossible, the incomprehensible, the illogical, and we do not. These pointed, unanswerable questions bring Job back to his spiritual senses, and he responds with worship. He says to God, "I know you can do all things and no plan of yours can be thwarted. Surely I spoke of things I did not understand, things too wonderful for me to know." Job moves from confusion and anger at his own circumstances to a focus on a powerful and mysterious God.

The story of Job is both awful and wonderful. Here, we see a broken man in pursuit of the sacred. In the midst of unspeakable personal tragedy, Job chases after God. Emotionally and spiritually, Job is a mess. But he knows the answers lie with God. He knows he must move towards God and not away from God. He demands to know why he, a good and righteous man, has been targeted with such loss and destruction. He demands a meeting with God. He pursues God with a heartbroken edge. He is filled with anguish and pain and confusion and anger. Job reminds us death and loss are messy business. Job pursues the Divine in order to make sense of his tragic losses. And God meets him in a most remarkable and life-changing way—not with answers but with himself. He turns Job's focus from "why" to a focus on God—a focus on that which is sacred and holy and beyond knowing.

Real tension exists in the pursuit of the sacred: Why is this happening? What's going on here? What is the Spirit of God saying? Real tension exists in the ultimate submission of Job to God, who knows so much more than he does. Job does not shy away or turn off or shut down. But neither does he get hard and bitter. Job remains receptive to God's love, and in the end he sits in humble reverence.

When we are faced with inexplicable loss and inconsolable grief, Job and the Bernardos remind me there are many things I do know.

> I know that my redeemer lives, and that in the end he will stand on the earth. And after my skin has been destroyed, yet in my flesh I will see God; I myself will see him with my own eyes—I, and not another. How my heart yearns within me!
> —Job 19:25-27

What do I know? If God never did another thing for us, it would be enough. He has already given us life by sending his Son. God has already declared his love for us through the sacrifice of Jesus. It is enough. If God never discloses to us why Geoff and Karen had to die, it is enough. It is enough he loves us and has given us eternal life. We will yet see God. And we will yet see Karen and Geoff. It is enough. I know in this world there will be trouble, incomprehensible trouble. And I know that I don't know why they died.

〜

Johann Christoph Arnold, the senior Elder of the Bruderhoff community, teaches that often the only appropriate response to inexplicable loss and tragedy is reverence: *What else could one do but stand in quiet reverence before such a sudden intervention of God?*[12] Here is a surprising response that needs to be pondered—a gift that needs to be held quietly, thoughtfully in our hearts. We can encounter the sacred in the midst of this silent reverence. With no answer to the agonizing question of why, there remains mystery. We must acknowledge we do not know and likely will never know. With more going on than we can possibly understand, we hold "the pain" and "the why" in reverent tension in our hearts. These are holy moments. God still meets with us and speaks to us. These are matters of the soul—deep loss stirs the very core of our being. These may be the holiest moments of our lives—times we simply sit in silence and ponder that which we do not know.

The death of a baby is accompanied by a unique sadness and futility that is different from the death of older children. Not easier or harder, just different. With a baby's death there is precious little to remember, but the loss of the future is immense. Arnold reflects:

> The birth of a baby is one of the greatest miracles of creation. . . . [T]he death of an infant, the birth of a stillborn baby, or the experience of a miscarriage is not only an event of great pain and sorrow, it is also a particularly hard test of our faith. One wonders, "Why did God create a child at all, if it was to live so briefly?" The thought that perhaps its brief sojourn here on earth carries a message from God's kingdom is an awe-inspiring one, but it does not necessarily lessen a parent's grief. Clearly we stand before a mystery that only God understands, and all we can do is hold it reverently in our hearts.[13]

Every time a child dies, the pain seems unbearable. I do not believe parents can ever get over it. The wounds never completely heal, and they will always walk with a noticeable limp. But I do believe substantial healing can and will come in time, in Jesus, in love. Despite the limp, they continue to walk. For the first year or two, each step reminds them of their loss. But every step is also marked by faith—faith that their loved one is safe, faith that there is life yet to live, real hope that there is still love to give and receive. In the midst of this limping, faltering, faith-assisted journey, healing begins to take hold. The excruciating pain slowly settles into an ache that will not be soothed.

I also believe that whenever a child dies, we stand on holy ground. There is something deeply profound and mysterious and sacred taking place. The world stands still; even the heavenlies seem strangely silent. Something shifts in the cosmos. I wonder what takes place in the realm of God and his angels. Do they cry? Are they busy preparing a welcoming party? How does heaven receive the souls of its youngest members?

Every time a child dies, part of us needs to remain open to the coming of God's Spirit—his presence, his grace, his love, his tears, his comfort, his mystery. Part of us needs to trust that God comes to us in the birth, life, and death of that child. There are great and terrible things to ponder here. When Mary gave birth to Jesus, after the shepherds had come to worship, we are told, "Mary treasured up all these things and pondered them in her heart" (Lk. 2:19). There was deep mystery here in the birth of Mary's baby that could only be held in silent reverence. Thirty-three years later, when Mary stood at the foot of the cross and watched her son die, I can only imagine that mixed in with the horror and the pain, there was some part of Mary pondering these events in her heart—a silent reverence born out of standing in the presence of sacred mystery.

Finding ourselves in a place of reverence seems like a strange gift. It is another aspect of the Christian life that does not make complete sense but feels absolutely right when we are in the middle of it. Sometimes silence and awe are the only appropriate responses. I find it remarkable that the initial response of Job's friends was to sit with him in silence for seven days. Seven days! It is hard for me to fathom such a pain-filled, yet absolutely right response. In the end, Job's friends proved to be poor comforters, speaking about things they had no knowledge of. It would have been better for them to leave after the seven days without a word—they should have just stood up and walked away.

> Even the most unlearned of men knows that the truly important matters of life are those for which we have no words. Yet we must speak of them. We speak, as it were, around them, under them, through them, but not directly of them. Perhaps the Master of the Universe thought it best not to give us those words, for to possess them is to comprehend the awesome mysteries of creation and death, and such comprehension might well make life impossible for us. Hence in His infinite wisdom and compassion the Master of the Universe gave us the obscure riddle rather than the revealing word. Thus we should give thanks to him and bless His name.[14]

EIGHT

Love

A FRIEND AND RESPECTED COLLEAGUE ALMOST DIED. He underwent life-threatening surgery, spent many weeks in hospital and six months later is still recovering. There were times when doctors were unsure he was going to make it. During his illness, my friend and his family received many and varied expressions of love. During his lengthy recovery, he wrote a letter to his community of support to express his gratitude:

> During this time we have been carried by the love, encouragement, and practical help of friends and family. The love of God was displayed to us in so many ways. Love washed my hair when I was too weak to stand. Love walked with me to the bathroom and pushed my wheelchair out into the sunlight (even though we were told not to leave the ward). Love was seen in an old friend who went out of his way to come by and a new friend who cared in unexpected ways. Love bought us a computer when ours was stolen. Love was a nurse who held my hand when I was afraid, sat in the waiting room for hours just to be there, and explained what was happening in words I could understand. Love covered a gym membership so I could regain my strength.
>
> Love gave us a cell phone when ours got lost in the chaos. Love cleaned our house, folded our laundry, and

walked our kids to school. Love was shown through a doctor who helped move up my surgery date by four months and another doctor who didn't just see us but also prayed with us in the examination room when the answers were not coming. Love was shown by elders who served us communion in our home and a church family who gave us a gift bag at Christmas to remind us we were part of a community. I have learned what Paul declares in his letter to the Romans that "nothing in all of creation is able to separate us from the love of God that is in Christ Jesus our Lord." And that love was shown through you.

Love is universally desired but, strangely, many never find true love because we do not know how to receive it or how to give it. We learn from an early age the nature of conditional love—a relationship based on some level of expectations and conditions, some level of *quid pro quo*: you do something for me and I will do something for you. This exists, to some extent, in every parent-child relationship, every husband-wife relationship, and in every friendship. People in conditional love relationships will always end up being disappointed. In reasonably healthy relationships, the disappointment will be occasional and the relationship will survive and perhaps even grow stronger as a result. In weaker relationships, the repeated disappointments will end in pain and anger and, sadly, in separation. We cannot succeed in meeting other people's expectations, and others will not be able to meet our expectations. Disappointment is inevitable.

My years of pastoral care and counsel lead me to believe moving beyond conditional love to the kind of true, unconditional love we all long for is rare but possible. One of the few places we find unconditional love is from our young children. They do not care about our day, our money, or our accomplishments. They just love us. We eventually teach them to put conditions on their love as we reward them for smiling, getting good grades, and being what we want them to be. But we can still learn a lot from the way children love us. True love finds its basis in who we are and not what we do or don't do. Young children love us because we love them. It's that simple.

The sick and the dying also catch a glimpse of true love when they find they are no longer able to reciprocate in any way. They are forced into receiving unconditional love. Most of us find it very difficult to receive an expression of sincere love without feeling the need to reciprocate in some way—to somehow even the score. Receiving something we cannot repay makes us uncomfortable. Why is that? Pride? A desire for independence? A sense of unworthiness?

Many of the sick and dying fight hard against receiving unconditional love, at least in the beginning. They tell people, "I'm quite okay getting along on my own, thank you very much. I'll call when I need something." They resist the gifts of love and support because they treasure their independence and do not want people to feel sorry for them.

I have seen the incredible relief and release that comes when the dying no longer fight the love that comes their way. It dawns on them that people really do love them without conditions. There is no *quid pro quo* here. They are not being loved because of what they can do in return, since their current state actually prohibits them from reciprocating. Yet the love keeps coming, washing over them like warm, gentle waves. And eventually they realize others love them for who they are. No strings. No conditions. What a wonderful gift.

God often sends us his unconditional love through the love of others. The two really are the same. When the sick, dying, and elderly accept and receive true love, something changes in their hearts. They, in turn, begin to love others more freely, more honestly, more completely. They no longer operate out of a conditional love paradigm. Many of the dying find love in ways they never thought possible. This helps explain why many of the dying say they would not change a thing about their current circumstances. Their dying has brought much love and joy to them. What a strange world we live in. It often takes the shadow of death for us to experience true love.

David "Mo" and Joanna rescue and love sick, starving, and hopeless children in Malawi, a country where drought, famine, disease, and death are sadly familiar. The death of children breaks their hearts, and I have often seen Mo in tears. If anyone has a good reason to stop loving so much, to stop caring so much, it's Mo. Given the unbearable pain that accompanies the death of each child, I would understand if Mo learned to withhold some of his love and established a self-protecting, professional distance between himself and the children of Malawi. Once, when he was talking about these children and crying so much he could hardly talk, I asked him, "How do you do it? How do you keep on going? How can your heart take it?" He said he asked the Lord to keep his heart tender, to not let it grow cold or calloused. He never wants to get to the point that the death of a child becomes tolerable. He never wants to stop loving and feeling. He takes comfort in knowing God loves every child more than he does. He finds strength in knowing God loves him even as his heart breaks.

The Trinity—Father, Son, and Holy Spirit—shows us how to love one another. Although existing in three distinct Forms, or

Personalities, they are One. The Father, Son, and Holy Spirit love one another intimately. They serve one another, defer to one another, uphold one another, support one another—they exist for the other. They cannot fulfill their purpose without the other. This models for us a mutual relationship of the highest and deepest order. We have been created in the pattern of, and in the likeness of, our Creator. We are designed for deep and intimate relationship based on loving and serving the other. At our core, we desire to give and receive love. God started the whole thing in motion by loving the other—that's us. We continue the process by loving others and by loving the Other—that's God. The goal is not for us to find someone to love us, but for us to love others. That is what completes us and makes us fully functioning human beings. The more we love others, the more human we are. The less we love others, the less human we are. When we begin to freely love others, love has a habit of taking us to places we could never have predicted or imagined for ourselves.

Our decisions to love or not to love shape who we are and have lasting impact. We have the potential to be as significant as our willingness to love others. And this love, the love that defines *who* I am, will outlive death. The grave cannot keep the love of God from reaching me. Death cannot stop the love I have for others. When widows talk about their love for their husbands, they talk about that love in the present tense. Death cannot in any way cancel the love that exists between two people. Jesus proved that to us.

When we love well, our loss will be profound. The pain is beyond description. But not even death can take our love away. When we have loved well and been loved well, those feelings of love go beyond the grave—they transcend death. When we have not loved well, death evokes not only profound sadness but also feelings of guilt, regret, and shame. That's when grief turns sour and begins to poison the soul.

Unconditional love is God's great gift to us. Every day, we can give that same great gift to others. We have within us the ability to give to others the thing they most desire and need. True love has the power to do so much good in the world. And when we choose to withhold it, we choose to stop doing good and we choose to bring harm.

I have found it refreshingly simple to love the dying. Loving the living seems to come with rules, expectations, and etiquette I find difficult to navigate. Loving the dying is most often reduced to the raw, basic essentials of tears, service, laughter, listening, and silence. Often, showing up is enough.

NINE

Peace

Praise God for all that's holy, cold and dark.

Praise Him for all we lose, for all the river of the years bears off.

Praise Him for stillness in the wake of pain.

Praise Him for emptiness.

Praise him for dying and the peace of death.

—FREDERICK BUECHNER[15]

M Y MOTHER'S DEATH WAS NOT PRETTY. MOM WAS ALWAYS
a worrier, and her worries seemed to magnify in her senior years.
She worried about the weather constantly even though she never
drove and was entirely housebound for the last many years of her
life. She watched the weather channel looking for bad weather to
worry about. She worried about her children and grandchildren,
but mainly she worried about being separated from her husband.
When my parents reached their 80s, their failing bodies regularly
led to periods of hospitalization, sometimes for just a day or two and
sometimes much longer. Whenever that happened, my Mom's fears
would escalate to the point of near panic. She had a hard time coping
when she was apart from my Dad. When my Dad fainted and fell,
something he did regularly for a season, Mom would panic to the
point of not being able to call 911. She did, however, always manage
to call me.

When my Mom fell and broke her ankle, I knew she was in
trouble. She was already close to immobile, only able to take a few

steps with a walker, and now she was completely bedridden. After two weeks in hospital, she was sent home with 24-hour personal support while we waited for a nursing bed to become available. We had known Mom would need full care soon, but now, with the broken ankle and with the likelihood she would never walk again, there was no option and no more discussion. Mom hated the idea of going into a nursing home. She was desperately afraid of being separated from Dad. After two difficult weeks of her remaining at home, we received a call on a Thursday that a bed was available; we made plans for the move on the following Monday. I dreaded what Monday would bring, but Mom had other ideas. She died on Sunday. She really did not want to go to a nursing home.

In the final two weeks, my Mom's failing mind began to fixate on her fears. Every conversation was the same:

I'm afraid.

Mom, there's nothing to be afraid of.

No?

No, you're going to be ok. Lots of people are looking after you.

They're not going to kick us out?

No one is going to kick you out.

I'm so scared.

Mom, there's nothing to be afraid of.

No? They're not going to kick us out?

My Mom barely survived the second world war. She lived with her mother, father, brother, and sister in what was then called Prussia. Her mother died in her arms after being shot accidently by a Russian soldier. Her father left the house one day and never returned. Her brother was killed in battle. She nearly starved to death. We know these bare facts, but we know nothing of her emotional and mental trauma because she refused to talk about those years. I suspect her obsessive fears later in life were not as irrational as they appeared to us.

In spite of her faith in God who loved her and her firm belief she would be with God upon her death, she desperately feared being left alone, without her husband. Her fear-filled season of dying was not easy to watch, not easy to be around, not easy to understand. I am grateful for her relatively quick death.

Joani, a dear family friend, faced her season of dying at the same time as my mother. Until being diagnosed with advanced pancreatic cancer, Joani was incredibly vibrant and active, happily invested in the lives of her children and grandchildren, and fully engaged in her community. Although her activity greatly diminished in her final year, she continued to be a lady of faith, wisdom, grace, and beauty. Joani and Laurence are two of our longest-standing friends. We have known each other for 30 years, and during those years we have celebrated many birthdays and anniversaries. They are honorary grandparents to our two very white, blonde, blue-eyed daughters. Joani and Laurence were born and raised in Jamaica and are, not surprisingly, black. During our elementary school years, Joani and Laurence often attended special school functions and watched proudly as our girls performed or presented. Their presence led to some confusion and amusement, especially when our daughters jumped into their arms and announced this distinguished Jamaican couple as their grandparents.

Doctors discovered a mass on Joani's pancreas that had wrapped itself around the colon, causing a painful obstruction. As Joani absorbed the news from the hospital doctor, she turned to her husband and asked, "Are you ok?" Joani was somewhat surprised at her own response to the news, but that unusual peace continued.

Within days of the initial discovery, Laurence sent family and friends a medical update and ended his email with, "Joani wants you all to know she abides in the peace of God which passes all understanding." A week later, after confirmation that the cancerous mass involved multiple organs, Joani reminded us the Scriptures tell us "*in* everything give thanks," not "*for* everything give thanks" (1 Thess. 5:18, KJV).

After multiple tests, scans, and appointments, doctors suggested surgery as a last-ditch effort to prolong her life and ease her pain. After attending a pre-op appointment in October, Laurence sent out an email with the verse, "I keep my eyes always on the Lord. With him at my right hand, I will not be shaken. Therefore my heart is glad and my tongue rejoices; my body also will rest secure . . ." (Ps. 16:8–9).

When doctors opened Joani up, they found the cancer had progressed too far, deemed her inoperable, and closed her up. She awoke to find her husband crying quietly beside her and doctors talking about palliative care. Joani's first response was to reach out for her husband's hands and comfort him with the words, "It's going to be ok."

I cannot help being inspired by Joani and Laurence's journey. Being able to watch as they worked out their faith and pain was a gift. In the face of their great crisis, they made a choice; in reality, they made many, many choices each day, but they made one fundamental choice. They chose to put their faith in God, and the result was an unreasonable peace, a peace beyond human comprehension.

In the midst of every emergency and crisis, there is a choice to be made—will we lean into God or pull away from God? That's a choice Mary, the mother of Jesus, made when faced with the mind-boggling news of her unexpected and impossible pregnancy. That's a choice parents make when a son or daughter is diagnosed with a life-threatening condition. That's a choice Joani and Laurence made every day as cancer relentlessly consumed Joani's body. Joani paraphrased Habakkuk 3:17–18, one of her favorite passages:

> Though the result of the surgical procedure is a huge shock and disappointment; though our hopes were dashed; though the confidence, trust, and assurance in my earthly doctors have been somewhat shaken; though I feel as if I am climbing up a cliff, no, a mountain, and the path is becoming more difficult; though tears flow freely, even as love grows deeper; yet I will rejoice in the Lord, I will be joyful in God my Savior!

Joani went on to say, "As we cross the desert, God has drawn me closer and closer to Himself. I have discovered flowers of Peace blossoming in the most desolate places."

Joani chose to lean into God and not pull away. She chose to believe that the God who walked with her when she was healthy was the same God who walked with her when she was desperately sick. Joani's circumstances constituted a real emergency, and in her season of dying she called out to her Father for help.

As we lean into God, we move from demanding, "Why me? Why this? Why now?", to "What have you got for me in this? What do I need to understand? What are you calling me to do, to be?" The *why* questions are entirely understandable, entirely human, entirely to be expected, but in the end they are, for the most part, unhelpful. They are "crazy-making" questions that cause our minds and emotions to run around in frenetic circles, as we try to make sense of circumstances and events that do not make sense.

Leaning into God causes us to stop focusing so much on the problem. When we encounter a crisis, our minds instantly fixate on the problem and all the implications—we are overwhelmed. We then go into problem-solving mode and become consumed with all the possible solutions. In the process, we lose sight of God. Joani's predicament was dire and her life was turned upside down, yet her focus was not on the chaos but on God. She did not simply *resign* herself to God's will, she actively *worshiped* God. Joani took great comfort in sitting down at the piano, with her limited strength, singing praises to her Lord and Savior. A month after the unsuccessful surgery, Laurence sent out a remarkable email to family and friends:

> For the last 30 minutes, Joani sat at the piano playing praise choruses and singing along. (I could have taken a picture to send but rather drank it in with Bible open.)
> To God be the Glory
> From Laurence (Dad)

When a problem begins to dominate our thinking, bring the matter to God. That sounds so easy, doesn't it? Whatever the problem or crisis, lean into God, inviting him to shed his light on the mess. This immediately puts some much-needed space between us and our concern, allowing the opportunity to see things from God's perspective. When we lean into God and consciously acknowledge his presence, the circumstances might not change, but our emotions and perspective sure do.

Joani still prayed for life but did so knowing her life was entrusted to a faithful, loving God. Joani still prayed for healing, but she was not fighting with God, demanding to know, "Why are you doing this to me?" and insisting, "You can't let this happen! You have to heal me!" She desperately wanted to live but acknowledged her living was subject to God's sovereignty. It was his call, not hers. And Joani did not stamp her feet and shake her fists demanding that God give her what she wanted. In her season of dying, Joani discovered an increased intimacy with God and understood the reality of Christ's words, "Peace I leave with you; my peace I give to you. I do not give to you as the world gives. Do not let your hearts be troubled, and do not be afraid" (John 14:27). Peace is a rare treasure, dazzling in delicate beauty yet strong enough to withstand all onslaughts.[16]

I don't know why my mother spent much of her life hampered by worry. I don't know why she spent her final weeks in a state of constant fear and confusion. No matter how hard we try, life and death do not conform to our expectations or desires. I am comforted by my father's picture of Mom in the moments after she died. My Dad spent 20 minutes with her before calling me, stroking her hair, touching her face, and holding her hands, and he talked about how her countenance was so completely altered. The worry lines were gone and the fear had evaporated. Dad said she looked twenty years younger. He was amazed at how peaceful and serene she appeared and concluded she must have seen Jesus. I am grateful for death's final gift of peace to my father and through him to me.

A few months after my mother died, I was preaching about death and dying in a nearby church. After the message, I invited comments and questions, and the first question came from a lady who tearfully asked why some people had such a hard time dying. A family member had recently passed away after weeks of physical and emotional agitation, fighting death every step of the way. There was no peace. I had a hard time answering her question. All I could think of was how hard it was to watch my mother die.

After the service, a different lady shared a picture she believed God gave her as this question was being asked and discussed. The picture was of a small, tired child fighting sleep. The mother of the child, knowing her baby needed sleep, was doing everything she could to comfort and console—rocking the baby in her arms, singing to her, soothing her with quiet words—and yet the baby kicked and screamed and fussed until eventually, exhausted, the baby fell asleep in her mother's arms. That picture brings me comfort.

TEN

Living Out
One's Call

I HAVE RECENTLY TURNED SIXTY AND OCCASIONALLY GET asked about retirement. That is a concept that does not entirely make sense to me because you simply do not retire from being a follower of Jesus. The dying regularly remind me of that lesson. You might retire from a job or a vocation, but you never retire from loving God and loving others. Although the way in which you carry out God's call may change with the passage of time, it takes an entire lifetime to complete. For many years before my mother passed away, she said she could not understand why God did not take her home; in the next sentence she answered her own question by concluding, "He must still have some purpose for me here on this earth." That is a sentiment expressed by many of my dying friends who say, at least I can still pray, or encourage my grandchildren, or read the Bible, or bless my kids.

Every human being has a call on their lives both generally and specifically. Each one is called of God to receive his love and enter into his peace. St. Augustine described this general call when he said at the start of his Confessions, "God, you have made us for yourself, and our hearts are restless till they find their rest in you."

And we have more specific calls that may last for months, years, or decades. We may receive many such calls in our lifetime. A friend of mine has a calling to write. He says he cannot *not*

write—it is something God has gifted and called him to do. I
have been called to be a pastor but did not sense that call until
I had completed a Master of Science in Forestry and embarked
on a career as a research scientist. Though my call to vocational
pastoral ministry has persisted for many years, God may yet shift
that calling to something new.

I confess that at times I struggle to keep true to my pastoral
calling. There are days when I would much rather curl up in a
chair and read a book or go for a long walk. Sometimes being a
pastor is too hard. Sometimes I do want to retire, at least for a
few days.

Not long ago, I met with a couple in their 70s. Susan and John were
full-time residents in a seniors care facility. John was recovering
from a stroke that left him completely mobile but without the
ability to speak. Susan was in the last stages of her battle with
cancer and was entirely bedridden. They had spent most of
their lives waffling between being indifferent to God and being
downright hostile. A family member had regularly asked Susan if
she might want a pastor to visit, and each time the answer was no.
But as the cancer advanced and the end drew near, she changed
her mind. The family member, someone I have known for many
years, emailed me and asked if I would be open to visiting with
Susan. She warned me Susan was in pretty rough shape physically
and John might be quite agitated by my presence—was I up for
the challenge? I felt I had to say yes but did so with considerable
hesitation: speaking with a dying woman I could do, speaking
with a dying woman whose husband might be openly hostile to my
presence was quite another matter.

We arranged a time for me to meet with Susan, and a few days later I was on my way to their residence. When I walked into the room, Susan was lying in her bed, eyes closed, seemingly sound asleep. She did not even stir when I entered. Her husband was nowhere to be seen. A nurse was sitting in the room at the foot of Susan's bed. I explained to the nurse who I was and that Susan had invited me to visit with her, but since she was asleep, it might be best if I came back another time. I was quite relieved to be on my way and avoid John in the process but, as I was talking, Susan opened up one eye and acknowledged my presence with a slight nod. It was clear to me she was not up for a conversation, and so I asked if she would like me to come another day. She nodded yes; even a single word seemed to be a challenge for her.

Satisfied I had done all I could, I said good-bye and turned to leave. I almost did leave, were it not for the nurse. This nurse, who had not said a word to me as I explained who I was and why I was there, suddenly said, "Since you're here you may as well pray for her." For those who have read *The Shack*, or seen the movie, this nurse bore a striking resemblance to Paul Young's God character, taking everything in but saying little. "Since you're here you may as well pray for her" were the words she spoke, but they seemed to come directly from God. It was as if I had just received a swift kick to my backside: "I've called you to be a pastor! What in the world do you think you're doing trying to leave without praying for Susan?"

Being the reluctant, way too cautious, overly polite Canadian pastor I am, I began to explain to the nurse I did not really have Susan's permission to pray, we hadn't even had our first conversation yet, and I wasn't even sure she wanted prayer. The nurse never said a word, simply arching an eyebrow as if to say, "So?" I felt entirely exposed, laid bare, by that one eyebrow.

I turned around and finally did something befitting my calling. I went over to Susan's bed, knelt down beside her, and uttered the first even remotely helpful words of the day: "Would you like me to pray for you?" And Susan whispered, "Yes." I was a little bit surprised but mainly relieved and asked, "What would you like me to pray about?" She said simply and honestly, "I don't know." I said, "That's ok, I'll just pray." I took her hand and prayed for her to know and sense the presence of God. I prayed for her to experience God's love. I prayed the peace of God would come upon her. And I prayed for her husband, John, who just about that time had come to the doorway of the room but had not entered. He seemed upset, but I carried on with my prayer. When I had finished, Susan appeared to be asleep, and I was not sure how much she heard or was able to receive. But then she opened her eyes. I asked if I could come back another time, and she said yes.

I got up to leave the room, and as I turned around, there was the nurse. I had forgotten all about her during my prayer time. I looked at her and she looked at me and she said, "Now, that's better." I felt like a 16-year-old being trained for his first job. There was no sense of criticism, no condescension, just an affirmation: "Now, that's better, that's what you came here to do." Was God speaking, or the nurse, or both?

I went out into the hall and introduced myself to John, explaining who I was and why I had come. Although he could not speak, he made it clear I was expected, and I got the distinct impression he was okay with my prayers. I told him I would come back when Susan was feeling better, and he nodded. He showed me some pictures of his extended family, and I recognized a number of them. We were having no trouble communicating, and after chatting for a few minutes, I said good-bye and began walking to the door of their unit.

As I reached for the handle, something inside of me, not the nurse this time, caused me to turn around, walk back to John and ask, "Would you like me to pray with you?" And to my surprise, he nodded yes. So I put my hand on his shoulder and prayed for him to receive God's love and to know God's very real presence. I prayed God would grant him peace, and I prayed for his dying wife. I prayed God would give him everything he needed to be the husband he was called to be in these final weeks. Halfway through my prayer, I noticed John was crying, and by the time I had finished he needed to find some Kleenex. I do not know what was going on inside of John, but God was at work breaking down barriers and softening his heart. I asked him if it would be okay for me to come and visit with him again, and he nodded.

Finally, I felt my pastoral responsibilities were complete and I left, somewhat chagrined, but mainly encouraged. I am quite confident the nurse heard everything that took place between me and John, and although she did not say it out loud, I imagine her saying, "Now, that's better."

I often reflect on my encounter with Susan, John, and the nurse, and see it as an encouragement and a challenge. These three, in their season of dying, remind me to be attentive to God's call on my life. What has he got for me today? Where is God at work in me and around me? And how am I to cooperate with his activity?

There is no better model for remaining true to God's call on our lives than Jesus. The Gospels give a good picture of how Jesus lived after he became aware of his death. In fact, the majority of the Gospel narrative describes how Jesus lived, served, healed, and taught after he became fully aware of his imminent death. In Jesus, we have a great example of living out God's call right to the end. Jesus continued to teach publicly and privately. He healed people and cared for those on the margins of society. He washed the feet of his disciples in a profound act of humble service. He prayed his high priestly prayers for his disciples and for all of us who would one day become his followers—the greatest prayers ever prayed. He went to great lengths to explain to his disciples what would happen after he died. He spoke of the state of the world, of the Holy Spirit, and of the trials and temptations coming their way. He spoke of their joy and victory in life and ministry and the amazing things they would end up doing in his name. He prepared them for life after he was gone.

In his final hours on the cross, Jesus took care of his mother. Seeing his mother and his friend John nearby, Jesus said, "Mom, it's going to be okay. You'll see. Go with John. He'll take care of you." "John, look after my Mom."

On the cross, with hours (perhaps minutes) left to live, Jesus listened to the confession of a common criminal and granted him new life. In his dying, Jesus continued to do exactly what he did when he was living.

When I asked Helen, "What changed in your life when you found out about the cancer?", she shared a conversation with her husband, Roy. She said, "Let's keep things as normal as possible as long as possible." Helen and Roy were already living out God's call on their lives. And they continued to do so as long as they could. They did not need to make a lot of changes now that Helen faced death. There was nothing splashy or dramatic about this, just a simple continuation of being faithful to God.

Helen's desire to keep things normal touches on a profound life principle: We live each day according to the love, grace, and strength God gives. Every day we submit to God's working in us and through us. Every day we depend on God. Every day God leads us. Every day we follow.

Many people discover a renewed call to prayer in their final years. Not only do they find themselves with more time to pray, but they also have much better discernment on how to pray and what to pray for. They live in rarified spiritual air. With their acute spiritual sight, soft hearts, and minds uncluttered by the cares of the world, I wonder what seismic shifts have occurred in the heavenlies because of the prayers of the dying.

I have many treasured memories of pastoral ministry—of caring and counselling, of prayer and healing, of deliverance and release, of reconciliation, of decisions for Christ, of baptisms, and of marriages. But I suspect the most profound acts of pastoral ministry were and continue to be my simple presence as friends and loved ones pass from this world into the next. As I remind the dying they are God's beloved and have fulfilled their earthly duties and are free to go, I know I am being the pastor God has called me to be.

ELEVEN

Character Upgrade

Sharon and Doug were happily married for 37 years. One night, Doug suffered a massive and fatal heart attack in his sleep. Over the next few years, I met regularly with Sharon as she tried to come to grips with her devastating loss. Two years after Doug's death, I asked Sharon what changes had occurred in her life. Sharon said, "I've become much more vulnerable and transparent. I'm able to talk about what's going on inside of me in ways I'd never done while Doug was alive. I used to put my best foot forward and put on my happy face most of the time. Now I have the freedom to be real, authentic, honest." This change in Sharon now allows her to come along side of others in ways she could not have imagined. Sharon says she has a deeper relationship with God. She is more sensitive to God's Spirit and hears him in new ways. As her faith grew more confident, so did her desire to tell others about Jesus.

Before Doug died, Sharon was able to do much in her own strength. But since Doug's death, her strength is gone—she is completely broken. And her brokenness has brought her into a deeper dependency on God. She recognizes the gracious gift of a God who walks right beside her in her journey of loss and grief. Sharon's deeper relationship with God was something she had longed for and prayed for. She did not want it to come this way, but she has accepted it as a gift.

And Sharon says, in a strange sort of way, she worries less now. She has come to understand what Jesus meant when he said, "Do not worry about tomorrow, for tomorrow will worry about itself" (Matt. 6:34). So she tries to be fully available to God in the present and not worry about what might or might not happen tomorrow. Sharon says, "I don't even know if there will be a tomorrow."

All of these changes have come out of Doug's death. Would she trade them all in to have Doug back? I think she would. But that is not her call. So, some of Doug's greatest gifts to his wife came through his death. Can you think of better gifts than to have one's relationship with God become deeper and more intimate, to worry less and be more fully alive and present each day?

Loss strengthens us and softens us at the same time. It makes us wiser and makes us more whole. Loss makes us more human and more humane. Loss chisels and chips away the rough, ragged edges of our lives, making it possible for the real person to emerge.

A number of years ago, our family spent six wonderful weeks in Europe. We had the privilege of seeing Michelangelo's *David* in Florence's Accademia Gallery. It is the single most breathtaking sculpture I have ever seen. The Accademia designed and built a special hall for the purpose of displaying *David*. As we rounded the corner of that hall and the statue came into full view, audible gasps came from our tour group. One of the gasps came from me. The larger-than-life statue was stunningly beautiful. Our passionate tour guide described *David* as Michelangelo's greatest work.

Apparently, Michelangelo did not consider himself a particularly gifted painter. He was first and foremost a sculptor. Michelangelo had a simple but profound approach to sculpting. When he received a large piece of marble to work with, he spent days studying the hunk of rock. He looked at it from every angle and also peered into it. He only picked up his hammer and chisel when he perceived in the marble the image already there.

Michelangelo's artistic genius lay in his ability to chip away the pieces that hid what was already there waiting to be released.

Leading up to the statue of *David*, on either side of the hall, are four impressive sculptures collectively known as the *Prisoners*. Each statue depicts a body in the process of being freed or released from the marble rock holding it. The *Prisoners* provide dramatic testimony to Michelangelo's artistic process.

As we confront loss and death, much of what keeps us from being authentic gets chipped away, sometimes rather forcefully. When we experience profound loss, when we stare death in the face, when we truly become aware of our mortality, when our heart breaks and our world begins to come undone—all of these function like the strokes of Michelangelo's hammer and chisel—a painful cutting away of pretense and a releasing of what is held within.

Ultimately, death releases us from the rock of our planet Earth and from our flesh-and-blood bodies and frees us more completely to become what we were always destined to be—spiritual and eternal. In the meantime, while we yet live, the losses of those we love do their preparatory work by stripping away that which is unnecessary and false, leaving the good and true. In the midst of the loss, it is hard, perhaps impossible, to see how we have grown. Only in looking back can we see an upgrade in our character.

> Therefore, since we have been justified through faith, we have peace with God through our Lord Jesus Christ, through whom we have gained access by faith into this grace in which we now stand. And we boast in the hope of the glory of God. Not only so, but we also glory in our sufferings, because we know that suffering produces perseverance; perseverance, character; and character, hope. And hope does not put us to shame, because God's love has been poured out

into our hearts through the Holy Spirit, who has been
given to us.
—Romans 5:1–5

Paul has an unpopular response to suffering and loss. He says
we can *glory* in our sufferings. Suffering can lead to good things
and in the midst of the suffering we can rejoice and be thankful. And lest we dismiss him as naive, we need to know Paul had
amassed a significant resume of suffering over the years:

> I have worked much harder, been in prison more
> frequently, been flogged more severely, and been
> exposed to death again and again. Five times I received
> from the Jews the forty lashes minus one. Three
> times I was beaten with rods, once I was pelted with
> stones, three times I was shipwrecked, I spent a night
> and a day in the open sea, I have been constantly on
> the move. I have been in danger from rivers, in danger
> from bandits, in danger from my fellow Jews, in danger
> from Gentiles; in danger in the city, in danger in the
> country, in danger at sea; and in danger from false
> believers. I have labored and toiled and have often
> gone without sleep; I have known hunger and thirst
> and have often gone without food; I have been cold
> and naked. Besides everything else, I face daily the
> pressure of my concern for all the churches. Who is
> weak, and I do not feel weak? Who is led into sin, and
> I do not inwardly burn?
> —2 Cor. 11:23–29

We should listen to Paul: he is no ivory tower preacher. He
comes to us with the marks of pain and loss and death all over

his body. He knows what he's talking about. Paul looks back over his eventful life with gratitude and with rejoicing, not at the suffering he endured, but at what the suffering produced in him. His character improved over the years. He became a better person. Paul testifies his suffering produced in him perseverance or endurance. He is a stronger person. He is able to endure more, just as fire tempers steel, thereby increasing its strength, or as the athlete who trains (suffers) daily so she might become faster and stronger.

Suffering and loss, much like discipline and training and correction and reproof, have the potential of producing good things in our lives; they help us mature. We can be trained by our suffering so that a good outcome results. Are suffering and loss, then, tools of God to make us into the kind of person he wants us to become? Does he send death and loss our way? Does somebody I love dearly have to die in order for me to become a better person? These legitimate questions deserve a clear response. Often the dying and grieving suffer needlessly at the sincere words of confused men and women who seek to explain why suffering occurs. They, like the friends of Job, speak of things they know not.

God is not the author of evil, but he may allow it. God takes what was meant for bad and turns it in such a way that good results. God does not promise to shield us from loss, suffering, heartache, and death, but he promises never to leave us nor forsake us. He will walk with us in the midst of the pain. Suffering does not mean that God is angry with me or that he has given up on me. It is better to quietly ponder the mysteries of God than to dwell on the question, "Why is this suffering taking place?" The best answer to "Why?" is often "I don't know."

God speaks to us in days of sunshine and in days of rain and in days of torrential downpours. Thousands of years of human history tell us we tend to be more open to hearing God in the downpours. We should not blame God for that reality. We learn more from a loss than we do from a gain. This is a painful truth. Sorrow and loss often reconfigure our view of the world in a way that brings us closer to reality. We never know the complete story. There is always more going on in the midst of suffering and loss than we are aware.

Seasoned veterans have a lot more wisdom and endurance than untried rookies. In my early years, I avoided anything to do with death because of fear and not knowing what to do or say. I do not do that anymore. My capacity to persevere in the face of death is greater now than 20 years ago. And that is true of other painful situations as well. What used to unsettle me or cause me to react in fear, anger, or frustration does not impact me as much these days. Of course, I speak in relative terms here. I am heading in the right direction but have by no means arrived. Lots of things still cause me to react in unhelpful and unhealthy ways, but they are fewer and less frequent and do not last as long. This is a life-long process.

Paul continues by saying endurance produces character. God is more interested in our character than in our being happy or famous or rich. Loss provides a painful but much needed upgrade to our character. We become softer in the areas that need softening, such as compassion and empathy and love. We become harder (deeper, stronger) in the areas that need hardening, such as courage, taking risks, coming alongside of the hurting, being there when we are needed.

Paul finishes by saying his upgraded personality includes hope. Why is it some of the most hopeful people are those who have suffered the most devastating loss? Why do the dying often manifest more hope than the living?

A quiet, resolute, unshakable hope resides in many of the dying. Strangely, the dying often bring comfort to their caregivers by sharing with them their hope in God, who will never leave them. I do not think the dying ever give up hope of healing, but at some point hope transitions from a physical healing here and now to a more complete and longer-lasting healing. Either way, they are going to be okay.

The hope of the dying and the hope of those who suffer through incomprehensible loss lies in the very real love of God. God is real. God's love is real. Hope knows, in the end, even in the midst of pain, and maybe especially in the midst of pain, that there is still love. Love makes certain the promise of a good outcome.

My friend Jeff says the belief God will not give you more than you can handle is a myth. He says we regularly experience more than we can handle. And in the process, we learn things we could never learn otherwise. We learn about vulnerability and dependence on God. We learn to pray. We learn humility. We learn we are not God. We get wiser. We become more compassionate. We gain courage.

Jeff is right. I also want to affirm, "God is faithful; he will not let you be tempted beyond what you can bear. But when you are tempted, he will also provide a way out so that you can endure it" (1 Cor. 10:13). These words from Paul have to do with the temptation to sin, but suffering and loss can sorely tempt us to sin. They cause us to doubt our faith, to doubt in the love of God. They cause us to harden our hearts and build around us all kinds of defensive barriers. We become bitter and angry. So Paul's words are applicable to our discussion.

Jeff and Paul say much the same thing. In the midst of the suffering, we feel that we simply cannot handle it. And if we dare to think about it ahead of time, we absolutely know we will not be able to handle it. Who can imagine "handling" the loss of a child or a spouse? That is unthinkable. But people who suffer devastating loss *do* get through it. God promises to remain faithful in the midst of the trials. He promises to be present. And if we are attentive to the possibilities, we learn so much in the midst of suffering that we cannot learn elsewhere.

The most difficult challenges of life shape our character. In some, suffering and loss produce bitterness and despair. In others, like the widow Sharon and the apostle Paul, they yield authenticity and strength and hope and compassion. God can use the worst of times to do some of his best work if we are open to his presence and his love. The end of our journey remains certain; the quality of the journey is still in question.

TWELVE

Simplicity

My Father is 85 years old, and over the last few years, he has been teaching me about simplicity. This has been a startling journey to witness. Not so long ago, my Dad worked full-time, drove a car, maintained a modest four-bedroom house, looked forward to a hot home-cooked meal every evening, watched TV, participated fully in his local church, volunteered in the community, and helped raise four children. By all societal standards, his life was full and productive. Over the years, my parents downsized from a house to a town-house to an apartment to an even smaller apartment. Each step required shedding an alarming amount of furniture, books, magazines, pictures, toys, tools, and household equipment, not to mention clothes and shoes. Each step required an intentional move toward simplicity. Ten years ago, any semblance of formal cooking stopped. Five years ago, my Father sold his last car to the junk dealer. Last year, Dad decided he no longer needed access to the Internet. Two weeks ago, his wife of 61 years passed away. Life has become profoundly simple. What I find startling is how my father navigates each step towards simplicity with such grace. He does not want more. He is quite content with less.

For many of us, tomorrow holds the promise of more excitement, more love, more money, more power, and more toys. This pursuit of *more* keeps us in a constant state of feeling incomplete. We know by experience that every time we get what we want, we still are not satisfied. In fact, the failure to fill the emptiness just makes us feel worse. *More* does not complete us, and, in pursuing more, we become increasingly disillusioned and desperate.

The dying challenge me with the words, "I have enough. I don't need more stuff. In fact, I don't want more." Could I affirm these sentiments? I have no trouble hearing them, maybe even agreeing with their rightness, but could I declare them for myself and actually mean them?

In his book *Love Is Stronger Than Death*, Peter Kreeft recalls the Latin rite for the burial of an Austrian emperor in which the people carry the corpse to the door of the great monastic church. The door is locked. They strike the door and say, "Open!" The abbot inside says, "Who is there?" The people reply, "Emperor Karl, King of Austria." The abbot says, "We know no such person here." They strike the door again. "Who is there?" "Emperor Karl." "We know no such person here." They strike a third time. "Who is there?" "Karl." And the door is opened.[17]

You cannot take any of it with you. You only take you.

Being content with what we have allows us to truly live in whatever situation we find ourselves. We do not need more to be happy and content. We have enough now. I have been fortunate enough to do some mission-related travel over the last few years, visiting some very impoverished regions of the world. I know what every other traveler to such regions knows: being content is not based on material wealth. Why does more joy and contentment exist amongst the poor than the rich? This has to be a gift of God. The apostle Paul understands this gift, for he has "learned to be content with whatever I have. I know what it is to have little, and I know what it is to have plenty. In any and all circumstances I have learned the secret of being well-fed and of going hungry, of having plenty and of being in need. I can do all things through him who strengthens me" (Phil. 4:11–13, NRSV). Many of the dying receive this same gracious gift. The dying, with so little time left, with diminishing capacity to care for themselves, with no power, are often more content than those of us who are actively (frenetically?) pursuing life. In saying this, I don't want to romanticize death. The dying do not want to die—they want more time with their loved ones, more time to attend a graduation or a wedding, or to witness a birth. But their material pursuits change dramatically.

The dying simplify their lives. With little energy for complexity and no desire for excessive external stimuli, they, instead, look for peace with God and peace from God. They look for joy in relationships and live for a simple touch, a hug, a kiss. Content with good, honest conversation, they dwell on the important, not on what seems urgent to others. No need for gamesmanship, no more hoops to jump through, no more accolades to receive, no more bonuses to fight for, no more toys to covet, no more rungs on the ladder to climb. But there are relationships to cherish and make right, words of love and forgiveness to be spoken, memories to share and new memories to make. There is still time for laughter. There is life yet to live.

THIRTEEN

Celebration and Playfulness

But we are not without hope, for it is because we are so empty, having used the last scrap of our own resources, that God can move in. To work on us, and even to play. Even our bitter emptiness gives God room to play, as at the creation, placing whales in the sea and humans on dry land, then bringing all the animals to Adam to see what in the world he will call them. This is not imposed merriment, but of genuine delight and joy.

—KATHLEEN NORRIS[18]

CATHY WAS IN THE FINAL WEEKS OF HER LIFE. She had recently been moved to a hospice—a place that offers great attendant care, a setting of much grace and peace. Cathy knew she would die in her hospice bed at some point in the near future. But Cathy wanted to party. Her husband was turning 60, and not only did she want to ensure he was celebrated, she wanted to celebrate with him. And so, with the help of family and friends, Cathy planned her husband's sixtieth birthday party. A small guest list was prepared, food and drinks were organized, along with decorations, and, of course, a cake. Cathy insisted in getting out of bed, getting dressed, having her hair combed, make-up applied—the whole bit—and then she sat in a chair for two hours so she could be right in the middle of all the festivities. She laughed and talked and sang Happy Birthday along with the rest of us and she ate cake. We all knew the party was as much for Cathy as it was for her husband. She died a week later.

In my early years of coming alongside the dying, I remember being regularly surprised at the laughter, the jokes, and the playfulness of our encounters. I came to these visits with a certain amount of heaviness—a gravitas that seemed to me to fit the occasion. These were, after all, dire circumstances. Who would dare laugh about death and cancer and palliative care? It turns out that the dying would. Laughter is often a welcome visitor in meetings with the dying. Don't misunderstand me—profound sadness remains close by as bodies waste away, but a sweet joy regularly makes an appearance. The dying still love a good story or a good joke. They still love to laugh. They still desire to celebrate life. They poke fun at their disease and their condition in a way that chases away the heaviness. Many times, the dying make me laugh. Consistently, I would leave my time with the dying feeling a little lighter than when I arrived. When Cathy was diagnosed with incurable cancer, her husband promised to make her laugh every day. Shortly before she died, Cathy told me he had been true to his word.

In this world, life and death, joy and sadness arrive in close proximity. When you celebrate the wedding of a son or daughter, you participate in a new beginning as well as a departure. Tears of joy mingle with tears of loss, as you realize your child no longer belongs to you. Similarly, when we celebrate death, we cry over lost friendship and rejoice in the departed one's newfound freedom. Within minutes of Dave's death, his daughter Meghan, through her tears, pictured her father doing cartwheels in heaven. And we began to laugh in the middle of our crying. What an awesome picture! This man who could not lift a fork to feed himself, cartwheeling across the heavenlies.

Our sorrows and our joys co-exist in the celebration of life's many transitions. We experience tears of loss in the midst of weddings and the joy of freedom in the midst of funerals. Living and dying appear as dance partners alternating in taking the lead. So how do we prepare to celebrate death? By understanding what Paul told the Thessalonians:

> But we do not want you to be uninformed, brothers and sisters, about those who have died, so that you may not grieve as others do who have no hope. For since we believe that Jesus died and rose again, even so, through Jesus, God will bring with him those who have died.
> —1 Thesselonians 4:13-14, NRSV

Good news resides in the midst of sadness. Hope smiles in the midst of grief. We celebrate a death because out of this world's physical death comes the hope of eternal life. Death reminds us of eternity: every time someone whom we dearly love dies, eternity becomes more real to us. We think about it more. We anticipate it more.

To talk about death and celebration in the same sentence seems incongruous and wrong—but this concept comes together in a most profound way in the context of baptism. For followers of Jesus, baptism declares we have made the sincere decision to live the life of a Christian, that is, to be a Christ follower, and put our faith and trust in a God who loves us and forgives our sins. At some churches, baptism takes place in a baptismal tank, much like a very small pool. The waist-high water allows the one being baptized to go completely under the water and then rise up out of the water—a simple and powerful symbol of death and resurrection. As we go under the water, we identify with Christ in his death by a death of our own—a death to our old, sinful life, a life apart from God. This death of ours causes celebration, not mourning. It connects us with Christ. It connects us with all the believers who have come before us and will come after us. And so we have death and celebration in the same event. When we come up out of the water, a picture of cleansing and renewal, we identify with Jesus as he rose from the dead to a new life. And as the one being baptized comes up out of the water, the community of faith breaks out into applause and cheering. Time to celebrate!

When we begin to understand life and death, sadness and celebration actually do belong together, we gain a fresh understanding of one of the most perplexing sayings of Jesus: "For whoever wants to save their life will lose it, but whoever loses their life for me will find it" (Matt. 16:25). We end up discovering and celebrating a new life by losing our old one.

The writer of Ecclesiastes declares that weeping and laughing, mourning and dancing all have their time. Too many of us spend more time weeping and mourning than we do laughing and dancing. No doubt, our lives will be filled with enough heartache. But will our lives be filled with enough celebrations—both big and small? Do we celebrate the passages of life with family and friends, such as a child making the honor roll, or graduating from grade eight, or getting a B+ on a school project? Do we celebrate anniversaries and birthdays, and getting a promotion? Do we celebrate teenagers entering university or getting their first job? Do we celebrate when personal goals have been achieved? Do we celebrate the accomplishments of friends and family for no other reason than that we love them and are happy for them?

How will we be able to celebrate death if we do not know how to celebrate life? How will we be able to handle the final passage of life to death if we have not practiced on some of the less dramatic passages that occur throughout our lifetimes? If we do not know how to celebrate here on earth, how are we ever going to manage in heaven?

So, it's okay to play with someone who is gravely ill. The dying and those who love them still need to laugh. Playfulness can be expressed in so many different ways—sharing stories, laughing about silly circumstances, singing favorite songs, going out for dinner, watching a video in front of a fire, reading out loud, cooking a favorite meal, playing a game, or doing anything else you enjoy.

The dying realize, sometimes too late, the importance of play in all aspects of life. Life becomes more alive when we play, more meaningful and enjoyable. A little bit of play does wonders in changing our outlook on life. Play lifts our spirits and chases away the darkness of the day. Play keeps us young.

Many scientific studies have shown laughter and play reduce stress and trigger the release of substances in the body called endorphins, which are chemically similar to morphine. These natural painkillers and mood elevators may be why we feel better after laughing and playing: they give a natural high to our lives.

In his last year of living, Dave arranged to have a pool put in his back yard. He designed the pool and the landscaping, and he hired and managed the contractors—all from his bed and wheelchair. In many ways this did not make a lot of sense. But by building the pool, Dave communicated to his family it was okay to have fun after he died. And the backyard pool has provided the setting for many parties, much celebration, much silliness—around the pool Dave built just before he died. Just for fun. At the beginning of every summer since Dave died, Lorie invites a group of friends over for a party. There is much laughter, good food, good drinks, and the celebration of life, summer, and long, enduring friendships. At these parties, I often think about Dave. Good job on the pool, my friend. Cheers!

FOURTEEN

Time

STRANGELY, DEATH BRINGS WITH IT THE GIFT OF TIME. Death greatly diminishes our remaining time, making it more precious. Death sharpens time's focus and brings increased value to something we all take for granted. But the gift death brings goes beyond this. In death and dying, we discover an entirely new dimension of time. The very nature of time changes for the dying.

The Greeks, in whose language the New Testament of the Bible was written, used two significantly different words to describe their understanding of time. In today's English language, we lose something important in describing both of these concepts with the single word *time*. The first Greek term, *chronos*, means time in motion. It speaks of the future becoming the present and ending up as the past. It is "clock time" inclusive of seconds, minutes, hours, weeks, months, seasons, and years based in the rotation of the earth on its own axis and the movement of the earth around the sun. *Chronos* time is sequential and ordered in defined, cyclical, repeatable patterns. After night comes the morning, followed by the afternoon and the evening, and then the cycle begins again. We wake to the alarm, stumble to the bathroom, have our shower, get dressed, get the kids up, eat breakfast, drive the kids to school, drive ourselves to work and sit down at our desk. We wear wristwatches and carry smart phones and a host of other personal organizers, all of which are based on *chronos* or chronological time.

As a quantitative concept, *chronos* is measured time.

But *chronos* time does not truly exist in the way most things exist. We cannot touch it, see it, smell it, or hear it. And if we think about it, *chronos* time is made of things that don't exist anymore (the past) and other things yet to come into existence (the future). In reality, the only thing we can measure is time already past and gone forever.

The Greeks used another term, *kairos*, to denote an entirely different dimension of time. Its meaning cannot be captured in a single word or even a single sentence. It is alive time, dynamic time, now time, "just the right time" in which the decisive action takes place. It is the moment of monumental change at which the quintessential action takes place and ensures the desired result is achieved. It is qualitative rather than quantitative. It has no dimension but it has enormous significance. It is always *now*–not the past and not the future, but now.

The Bible uses *kairos* to describe those times when God's divine purposes intersect and overrule our chronological time–when God steps out of eternity and enters our time to ensure his purposes are achieved. The same word, *kairos*, describes those times when we, men and women and children, step out of *chronos* time and take decisive action with eternal consequences. *Kairos* is incredibly exciting and dangerous and profound. In these moments, we are fully alive.

The central *kairos* moment in human history is the life, death, and resurrection of Jesus.

> But when the fullness of *(kairos) time had fully come,*
> God sent his Son born of a woman, born under the
> law, in order to redeem those under the law, so that we
> might receive adoption as children.
> —Galatians 4:4–5, NRSV, emphasis added

> And he made known to us the mystery of his will
> according to his good pleasure, which he purposed in
> Christ, to be put into effect when the *(kairos)* times
> reach their fulfillment—to bring unity to all things in
> heaven and on earth under Christ.
> —Ephesians 1:9-10

The "fullness of time" language used by Paul is the biblical definition of *kairos* time. When the time is right or full, God moves. In a *kairos* moment, a seismic shift occurs in the cosmos. Never will things be the same. The world changes forever because, in the fullness of time, God sent his Son to us. God forcefully entered *chronos* time to accomplish his *kairos* purpose.

In the second letter to the Corinthians, Paul quotes from the prophet Isaiah, "In the time of my favor I heard you, and in the day of salvation I helped you." And then Paul states, "I tell you, now is the time of God's favor, now is the day of salvation" (2 Cor. 6:2). At the right and favorable (*kairos*) time, God hears and helps. And Paul emphatically states *now* is the most favorable (*kairos*) time and *now* is the day of salvation. The only time we can ever really seize is the now. Now is the time of enormous opportunity. Now is the time to seize and lay hold of eternity. Now is the time to believe in God, to change our lives forever by allowing Jesus to guide and direct and empower our ongoing "now."

Unlike the *chronos* time of past and future, *kairos* time of now really exists. In fact, only *now* time exists. *Kairos*, present and ongoing, appears as an icon of eternal life—an everlasting *now*, which contains no sequence, no before and no after.[19]

Arthur Boers recently wrote a wonderful book, *The Way is Made by Walking*, chronicling his 500-mile pilgrimage known as the Camino de Santiago. Arthur's destination was a cathedral in the city of Santiago de Compostela in northwest Spain. Arthur's long walk and his subsequent writings have helped me understand *kairos* time more fully. Arthur does not discuss *kairos* time specifically, but he lived *kairos* time for much of his journey. Although there was a stated objective in mind and goals of how far to walk most days, the intrinsic beauty and significance of the pilgrimage lay in the walking itself and in the people met and befriended and in God, who companioned him every step of the way.

In his book, Arthur introduces us to Albert Borgmann, a social philosopher and teacher deeply informed by Christian faith. Borgmann speaks of four focal affirmations he uses regularly to discover God's grace even in the midst of challenging times:

> There is no place I would rather be.
> There is nothing I would rather do.
> There is no one I would rather be with.
> This I will remember well.

Borgmann then asks the penetrating question, "When was the last time you were able to affirm these statements?"[20] The answer might be the last time you were in *kairos* time and not subject to *chronos* time.

> The saint in contemplation, lost to self in the mind of God is in *kairos*. The artist at work is in *kairos*. The child at play, totally thrown outside herself in the game, be it building a sand castle or making a daisy chain, is in *kairos*. In *kairos* we become what we are called to be as human beings, co-creators with God, touching on the wonder of creation.
> —Madeleine L'Engle[21]

God places us in *chronos* time, but we were made for eternity. We actually were not made for *chronos* time. Does that explain why so many feel we are prisoners to our schedules?

God places us in a physical body, but we are spiritual at our core and we long to be freed from our physical restrictions. We were not made to die, we were made to live forever. Is that why we have such a hard time comprehending our own death? It makes no sense to us. It is not what we were made for.

In her essay *Time by Design*, Linda Breen Pierce argues that time can be dead or alive.[22] Both Pierce and my friend Arthur suggest that driving has the potential to be dead time. Whether you are fighting through traffic in the soul-killing boredom of the daily commute or moving so quickly that you simply cannot process all that is happening around you, driving is an activity that is almost always merely a means to an end. In contrast, "live" time is worthwhile in itself. For Arthur Boers and many others, walking is an opportunity to enter into live time. In walking, the means is as valuable and worthwhile as the goal itself.[23]

When people face the thought or knowledge that they might die, they tend to move from dead time to live time. It is like the difference between driving and walking. Driving exposes us to both faster speeds and greater stimulation than walking. There is too much to take in, and so we shut down or we edit what we take in. We cannot take in all the scenery, all the beauty, all the information, all the danger, and so we typically focus on the danger and miss most of what goes by. When we are walking, everything slows down physically, to be sure, but also mentally. As we walk, we can process more of what we see. We have the time to absorb much more of the scenery: the flowers in the garden, the trees on the boulevard, the clouds in the sky, the cardinal in the bush, the toddler on the porch, the sound of cicadas high up in the trees. We actually have time to see and hear and experience more of life.

The dying quickly learn that each hour, each event, each kiss, each conversation holds its own profound relevance not to be missed, not to be rushed. They learn to be fully present. Two years after the sudden death of her husband, I asked Sharon what encouragement she might have for keeping relationships vibrant and alive. Here's what she said:

> Cherish each other in the little things—when your spouse dies you will not remember or care about the silver bracelets or the gold necklaces. But you will remember holding hands, and cooking dinner together and evening chats on the deck.

Many times, I am far from being fully present. My head and heart are otherwise occupied, even while the people I love the most sit next to me trying to have a conversation, trying to be in relationship. I analyze the past, plan for the future, and miss the present. We learn the lesson of being fully present much too late.

After Randy's wife died, we met regularly to talk about life and death. He carefully read every chapter of an early manuscript of this book and gave me candid, helpful feedback. Randy tells me that an ongoing effect of encountering death has been to notice the flowers more, to be aware of colors, to appreciate the kind and dear moments in life, to acknowledge the sunshine, to be more grateful when nothing hurts and to be much more conscious of his children's passage from childhood to adulthood. Days are richer and life is more vibrant. Randy is much more present these days. Death can be harsh and healing at the same time. Death takes life and gives life.

The birth of a baby is a *kairos* moment. A profound change takes place and the world will never be the same. The exact time of birth (*chronos* time) is but a marker and lacks any real significance compared to the *kairos* event. A new life enters the world and new dreams are born. We have good reason to rejoice—God yet again enters our time in the form of a baby, and the possibilities are endless!

Kairos time marks all truly significant, life-giving, and life-altering experiences. It is when we encounter God. It is when one person truly meets another person, even if just for a moment. Is it possible, then, that *kairos* time might be the unmeasured time of eternity? In heaven there will be no *chronos* time because there will be no future and no past, only now. In heaven there will be no devices to measure time because there will be nothing to measure. In heaven, it will never cross our minds to ask, "Where did the time go?"

If this is even partly true, then each and every *kairos* moment we encounter manifests a little bit of heaven here and now. We need not wait for death to enter *heavenly* time. It is available to us now—not in its fullest expression, but it is infinitely better than living in *chronos* time. Our *kairos* moments are tantalizing foretastes of what heaven is like.

The more time I spend with the dying, the more I realize the importance of simple presence. They have no desire to be impressed or entertained, and this means I do not need to be dazzling or funny, or have all the answers. But I do need to be fully present—listening, observing, taking in, caring, loving, feeling, crying, laughing—fully present right in the middle of the messiness of death. The gift we give to the dying is our self, our presence. Sometimes, that is all we have to offer and, often, it is all that is needed.

My dying friends regularly draw me into *kairos*. Being with men and women as they breathe their last is a most profound experience, a time when the sweep of the seconds loses its meaning. At the point of someone's death, time may not stand still (or perhaps it does), but it is somehow different. We are beyond time, outside of time, in *kairos* time. There is no agenda to keep, no schedule to consult, no chore to complete, no other person to meet. There is only this *event*, not marked by minutes but marked by the death of a lover, a spouse, a parent, a child, a friend—marked by a passing and a passage. The dying go where we cannot follow, and a new way of living awaits them. Their world changes forever, and so does ours. Every death occurs in the fullness of time. We do not die *before* our *chronos* time. When we die, it *is* our *kairos* time.

Celtic Christians believed in "thin places" where God is more accessible and more likely to be keenly felt.[24] Many of us, I would venture, experience thin places where we encounter the Holy, whether in a majestic mountain vista or in the eyes of an African orphan or sitting in a magnificent cathedral or holding a new-born child or standing in the presence of the desperately poor. And I would suggest that the spiritual air gets very thin when someone dies. There is a holiness and a sacredness to death. Heaven draws near.

FIFTEEN

Gratitude

Without death there would be no gratitude for
the life that we have been given.

—PETER KREEFT[25]

What's lost is nothing to what's found, and all the death
that ever was, set next to life, would scarcely fill a cup.

—FREDERICK BUECHNER[26]

I FEEL THE CUMULATIVE HEAVINESS OF MANY LOSSES. Too
many friends have died, too many funerals, too much heartache.
Too many people in their forties have died. That bothered me a lot
because I was in my forties when they died. Towards the end of that
decade of dying that I mentioned in the introduction, I attended
the funeral of young man killed in a tragic accident. I hardly knew
him, but I did know his parents. I sat rather rigidly through the
service, hiding the growing angst inside. I forced myself not to
connect with the pain in the room, fearing I would begin to cry
and never stop. I knew it was not the death of this young man that
threatened to undo me, sad though it was. It was all the deaths,
all the sadness that was about to spill out of me right then, right
there. It did not feel as if my life were falling apart, it felt as if *I*
were falling apart. When later I told my wife what I experienced,
she was quite surprised. My stoic exterior had communicated that
I was not emotionally connected at all with the tragic events of the
day. She thought I did not really care. In fact, I cared too much,

and found myself overloaded with unresolved emotions of loss and grief from the many years of death and dying.

My reaction to the death of a man I hardly knew prompted me to reflect more seriously on my previous losses. As I spent time with God reviewing, grieving, and crying, a surprising feeling began to emerge inside of me. I started to feel grateful. Not a lot, but enough to take notice. In the weeks that followed, as I quite intentionally reflected on the many losses, I became aware of more blessings. I know this sounds odd and feels strange for me to write, but I am fortunate to experience the sorrow of great loss. These feelings would not exist if I had not first experienced the joy of friendship and love. Over time, the losses are becoming bittersweet—a mixture of grief and gratitude. I am grateful for the deep and meaningful relationships with the people who have died. Those relationships are a gift from God.

If we are enjoying loving relationships, be they in our family or church community or in our place of work or neighborhood or among lifelong friends, we will experience great suffering and loss. This is inevitable.

The true value of anything in life is revealed most clearly by its absence. Absence is itself a form of death. We rarely take note of all the comforts provided by electricity. But when the power goes out, we are keenly aware of all we are missing. Most of us take our physical health and well-being for granted until we become sick or disabled. A loved one is never more appreciated than when they are gone. If we are rich in friends, we will experience our share of loss. If you feel you are suffering great loss, it is because you have been richly blessed by love.

It seems incongruous to be grateful when facing death, but death allows one to appreciate life in ways that the rest of us, who think we will live forever, can't or don't. Only in contemplating death are we jolted into a new appreciation of the now. Only from the perspective of death can we fully appreciate life, because the appreciation requires perspective and distance and comparison. Only from the air can we fully appreciate the land. Only after space travel can we fully appreciate planet Earth. Only after travel to other lands can we properly appreciate our country.[27]

Death frames life. Without an end, life on earth would lose its meaning. Death gives life its urgency, its drive, its passion. Death gives life its *life*. There is significance in life precisely because it does not go on forever.

Are we closer to one another in death than in life? Do we appreciate our loved ones more when the threat of death is upon them, or us? Is it possible that our senses are more heightened, more finely tuned to their love when their physical presence is gone? Do we take too much for granted when they are with us?

If you knew you had one last week with your loved ones, what would you do differently? How would you express gratitude and appreciation and love? What would you say? And why wouldn't you say it right now?

As Joani's appetite, weight, and energy slowly diminished, her awareness of and gratitude for natural beauty increased. Shortly before her death, Joani told me about her encounter with an amaryllis plant. The plant was a gift that was delivered after her cancer diagnosis. The plant itself was beautiful and the red flowers stunning. Joani would regularly find herself stopping as she walked past the potted plant just to admire God's handiwork. One day, she sensed God encouraging her to do more than just look but to reach out and touch the leaves, so she did. Her audible reaction was, "Wow!", as she felt the velvety smoothness. Prior to this, Joani could not remember ever taking the time to touch an amaryllis leaf.

Every time I talked to Joani, she mentioned the words grateful, thankful, and blessed. Given her inoperable, stage-four pancreatic cancer, this was rather surprising. As her health declined, she increased in gratitude. This seeming paradox is not unusual amongst the dying. One day, Joani summed up her journey with the profound and challenging words, "I am learning to be thankful for hard times and difficult journeys, trusting that God is accomplishing His best work through them. I am realizing that needing Him is the key to knowing Him intimately, which is the gift above all gifts. Every single thought and each prayer uttered on our behalf has been, and is producing indescribable joy and strength and encouragement, as we are surrounded and upheld with SO much love. WE ARE THANKFUL!"

Joani touches on a critical insight: Our need for and dependency on God is key to an intimate relationship with him, and this is nothing short of the most wonderful life-giving gift. Joani, in her desperate need of God, received the great gift of knowing him more intimately, and she was grateful.

I am both comforted and challenged by Joani's consistent expression of genuine gratitude. I am comforted that Joani experienced a level of divine contentment that superseded her circumstances, and I am challenged by my lack of gratitude in the midst of seemingly better circumstances. I am unable to utter a personal complaint in the presence of a dying friend. My friends are teaching me to be grateful for what I have, for things just as they are and not as I think they ought to be.

In their season of dying, my friends have expressed gratitude for family and friends and times when God was clearly present and actively at work. They are thankful for the years, however short or long, they have been given and are grateful for each new day, literally. They appreciate the smallest gesture of kindness: being driven to a doctor's appointment, having a meal dropped off at the door, a note of encouragement, a message left on their phone, a gift of flowers, being loaned a book, being served a cup of tea, being picked up for church. All these things produce in them surprising joy and well-being.

SIXTEEN

Guilt

A FRIEND CALLED AND ASKED IF I WOULD BE WILLING TO VISIT an elderly neighbour who was in hospital and likely in his last weeks. His wife had already passed away, and, although he had relatives still alive, most of them were at a distance. When I first met Paul, I saw a body that was failing but eyes that were still filled with life. I quite enjoyed our first conversation in which he gave me a quick sketch of his life, of his wife's death, and of his declining health. He was unlikely to leave the hospital alive. At our second visit, I engaged Paul in a discussion about death in general and more specifically about his own death: was he ready to die, was he at peace? His eyes went dark, and our conversation began to falter. It took a while to sort out and I never did get the whole story, but Paul was heading towards death filled with guilt and shame. I assumed the guilt had to do with unresolved issues with family or friends, perhaps even his recently deceased wife, but it turned out to be with God. Paul was terrified to meet God. When I asked him why, Paul said quietly, "You don't know the things I've done." Wracked with guilt, Paul was convinced that God wanted nothing to do with him and that there would be no welcome when he died.

Over the years, we accumulate a lot of life-related garbage, and many of us deal with this garbage by not dealing with it. We try to forget it or suppress it or get over it without actually doing anything about it. We think we have been successful when it no longer keeps us up at night or we stop crying about it. But most of this stuff just does not go away by itself. It slowly accumulates and causes interior damage even if we are not aware of it.

The effects are similar to a lifetime of unhealthy eating resulting in heightened levels of bad cholesterol. Although not noticeable from one day to the next, over the years our arteries become clogged, restricting the flow of blood and oxygen. This results in less energy, increased fatigue, and a substantially increased risk of heart attack or stroke.

We have hearts, minds, and spirits cluttered with a lifelong accumulation of unresolved relational debris resulting in a hardening of our hearts, a softening of our minds, and a dulling of our spirits.

Our doctor provides the much-needed wake-up call when our cholesterol reaches dangerous levels. The doctor says, "The news is not good. If you don't drastically alter your lifestyle you will be in serious trouble." And the doctor provides very clear instructions on what you can and cannot eat, how much exercise is needed, and what medication may be required. If it were not for the doctor's serious warnings, we likely would not change a thing. For many, the knowledge of impending death provides the necessary wake-up call to start dealing with the garbage that has accumulated.

Guilt is not a singular emotion, but a cauldron of negative, self-destructive, entirely unhealthy, and unhelpful feelings that lead to isolation and inner darkness. We feel *bad* and conclude that no one, including God, wants anything to do with us. We have done something horrible, and we just want to crawl into a hole somewhere and hide because we are ashamed. These feelings are not from God. They bring death to our spirit and our mind and sometimes even lead to physical death. They tend to isolate us and lead us away from the very sources of hope and healing most needed at a time like this—God and those who love us. The apostle Paul calls this "worldly sorrow" and states unequivocally that it leads to death. However, Paul also says that "Godly sorrow brings repentance that leads to salvation and leaves no regret" (2 Cor. 7:10). This "Godly sorrow" is part of our conscience, part of our sense of right and wrong, and is entirely healthy and helpful. This sorrow gets triggered when we know we have done something wrong, but instead of leading us into the black hole of guilt and shame, this sorrow prompts us to right action. God's Spirit guides us back to life, saying, "No, not that way—this is the way to go." Do not run away and hide; rather, confess your wrongdoing, ask forgiveness, and get back to living.

In truth, we *are* guilty and we know it, even if we do not like to admit it. I have found the dying to be brutally honest about this reality—not in a self-loathing way but in an objective reality kind of way. Consciously and intuitively, we know darkness resides inside of us. We are keenly aware of the things we would like to change about ourselves. We act wrongly, say things we wish we could take back, and think things that bring us shame. We are guilty.

> "I should really like to think there's something wrong with me—Because if there isn't, then there's something wrong . . . with the world itself—and that's much more frightening!"
> —Celia, in T. S. Eliot's play *The Cocktail Party*[28]

If God were to blame there would be no hope. If we are to blame, meaning if we are the ones who are weak and prone to making poor decisions, and if we are the ones who hurt one another, then there is yet hope in God. Our hope lies outside of ourselves.

Paul's fear of coming face-to-face with God upon his death was eventually overcome by his meeting with God while still physically alive. It took quite a while to convince Paul that God would not turn away from him no matter what he had done or not done in his life. Eventually, Paul agreed to make things right with God, whom he knew was all too real. Paul was not sure how to proceed and asked for my help. Still somewhat afraid but determined, Paul followed my lead and sincerely acknowledged his wrongdoings, asked for forgiveness, and accepted Christ as the One to follow for the rest of his days, however short those might be. Even in this final confession, Paul was unable to articulate the actions that caused him so much grief and guilt. He confessed in generalities, but I am quite convinced that God understood the specifics.

It sounds like a cliché even as I write this, but Paul's fear of dying disappeared that day. He accepted the fact that he was no longer guilty and he no longer felt guilty. He had made his peace with God and looked forward to his new life and death in Christ. I met with him one more time, a week later, and he told me with a smile on his face and a spark back in his eyes that he had called his brother and shared with him about his decision to "get right with God." He told his brother it was the best thing he ever did. Paul died the following week.

God's desire and capacity to forgive is so vast it approaches incomprehension. When we confess our wrong actions before God, we encounter grace. Even though we are guilty and might reasonably expect punishment, God offers forgiveness. Being loved by God in spite of our sin brings hope that we might receive love from others, even those we have hurt. They may not respond as graciously as God, although the majority of people are greatly relieved to hear our confession and will, in time, extend forgiveness. Reconciliation becomes a life-giving gift to the one who confesses and the one who forgives.

At times, the confession and request for forgiveness are met with anger, hurt, and bitterness. At this point, we can only pray for the other's healing. Having done our part, we must leave the rest in God's hands. Sincere confession to God brings his forgiveness and the removal of our guilt, but we also have to live with the consequences of our actions. Things do not automatically return to normal after reconciliation.

Although I have chosen not to include stories of guilt, confession, and forgiveness that the dying have shared with me over the years, I can personally attest to the life that results when issues of guilt are resolved. In the end, those who resolve guilt feel right again—rightly connected to God, to those they have hurt, to those they love, and to themselves. Reconciliation provides immense relief; the heart, mind, and spirit are renewed.

I have also witnessed the added pain and heartache that result when these issues are not addressed prior to death. Some of us prefer to take our secrets and our guilt to the grave. But when issues remain unresolved, we deny ourselves and the person we hurt the opportunity for healing and new life. By not dealing with hurtful actions, we end up refusing to accept a life-giving gift and also refuse to extend that same gift to others.

The kind of guilt discussed so far is based on very specific wrongs done to specific people. The dying express another kind of guilt as they come to grips with the end of their lives. I might call it regret. It is the general sense that our lives have been less than what they should have been or could have been. As the dying look back and review their lives, some feel regret for not being as loving, caring, and attentive as they could have been.

I have no single story to illustrate this but a collection of wistful emotions and nagging memories that add up to a sense of failure: too much time playing with things and not enough time devoted to people, too much emphasis on the destination and too little on the journey, too much money spent on themselves and not enough on others, too much effort trying to be loved and too little trying to be loving, too much time playing it safe. They should have gone to church more, should have prayed more, should have cared for the poor more, and loved their neighbor better.

Believing that their lives have, in some way, been deficient, the dying sometimes find themselves bargaining with God. They promise to turn their lives around if they are given a reprieve. They will dedicate their lives to doing good. They will go to church every week. They will be more loving. If God will spare them, they will become better people.

The dying put into words what many of us experience almost every day—a low level, nagging feeling of being less than we could be, less than we should be. I often have a sense of underperforming, believing that I should have done more and could have done better. I wonder if God will be pleased with me and conclude, how could he possibly be pleased with me? He's God. He's perfect. He's omniscient. There is no way he would be pleased. I imagine him tolerating me in the way a parent tolerates a young child who cannot be expected to accomplish anything worthy of note.

My dying friends have been helpful guides in dealing with this generalized regret precisely because they are unable to do anything about it. In their weakened states, they no longer have the option of working harder, longer, better. They have finished. The only thing left to do is to confront the feelings themselves and honestly and rationally assess what is worthy of remorse and regret and what is simply irrational and untrue. Together, with God, we figure out the things that need addressing and, if necessary, confessing, and then we take great comfort in the certainty of God's forgiveness. The rest we leave to God's grace and mercy.

SEVENTEEN

Forgiveness

As PART OF AN ON-CALL CHAPLAINCY SUPPORT for our local hospital, a group of pastors takes turns covering evenings and weekends when the full-time chaplain is not on duty. I don't get a lot of calls, but when I do, they always come in the middle of the night. The hospital called recently, and I was told a man in his fifties was dying and his family had asked for a pastor. The nurse who called warned me to expect quite a crowd. Even before I reached Eric's critical care room, I walked past six people in the hallway. There were easily another dozen people packed into the room. It took a while to figure out who they all were and who had called for me. The woman holding Eric's hand took charge and explained she was Eric's ex-wife. There was no current wife. I was introduced to Eric's son and daughter, who looked to be in their twenties. Also in the room were two of Eric's sisters, their spouses, and an assortment of nieces and nephews. According to Eric's ex, his life was marked by drug and alcohol use, violence, and prison. He was a physical wreck who had left a trail of relational debris far and wide.

Although Eric lay comatose, he still looked a little scary. Scarred and tattooed, with a scruffy beard and longish hair, he looked the part of an aging member of a biker gang. There was nothing pretty about this picture. Given the story, I was surprised and a little confused by the amount of emotion in the room. The daughter asked if she might have a few minutes alone with her dad, and we all filed out into the hallway. I could feel the tension and felt compelled to ask if there were any unresolved issues to deal with. I suggested that even though Eric could not respond, it was possible that he could still hear, and if any confessions or forgiveness needed to be extended, it was not too late.

The two sisters immediately began to cry, and one of the men standing close to me looked at me quizzically: "How did you know?" I asked the sisters if they wanted to spend some time with Eric. I encouraged them to make peace with Eric, not so much for Eric's sake, but for their own. As soon as the women entered the room, one of their husbands took me aside and explained that both sisters had been sexually abused by their brother and they had never forgiven him. He said that this was a crucial opportunity for his wife and her sister to bring some healing and closure to a lifetime of unresolved pain. When the sisters had finished, the rest of the family gathered around Eric and I led them in a time of prayer, release, and committal. Eric was dead before the prayer ended. I hope that Eric's sisters were able to forgive him.

Death often acts as a catalyst to navigate the life-giving waters of forgiveness. We have all been hurt, some of us in unthinkable ways. We carry the wounds and scars of living in a broken world. And we most certainly hurt others. We all know that hurt happens. Jesus acknowledged that in this world we will have trouble. The issue is not whether we will get hurt but what to do with that hurt. Many are unable or unwilling to get past the hurt. They cannot let it go. They cannot forgive. They cannot move on. This inability or unwillingness often leads to more damage than the original hurt.

There is no way out of this mess except through forgiveness. We need to forgive so that *we* can live whole lives. Forgiveness heals *our* hurts and wounds. Forgiveness reconnects us with others and ourselves. In the end, forgiveness is more about *us* than about the other. We need to forgive the other. If we don't, we become less human.

Forgiveness is the most loving and Godlike activity available to us. Forgiveness has immense power to heal and bring new life. When we forgive others, we image God in the profoundest of ways. God's love for us, and forgiveness of us, defines the core of his being. Love and forgiveness explain why and how God relates to us. To be human is to live out and express the image of God inherent within us. Therefore, we are most human, and most like God, when we love and forgive others.

Forgiveness recognizes that I am created in the image of God and that I have within me the God-given capacity and awesome power to forgive others. It also recognizes that the person who hurts me is, likewise, created in God's image. When I forgive someone, I acknowledge that God forgives me so much more. I do not receive what I deserve from God, and neither do I give to others what they deserve. Instead I give them what God gives me—forgiveness. The gift of forgiveness, not earned or deserved, comes from a heart of love. It is pure grace.

The dying may be able to work through forgiveness better than most because forgiveness is a form of letting go—and anyone facing death must let go again and again. When we do not forgive, we refuse to let go. And by hanging on to the hurt and anger, we allow those dark feelings to capture us. We allow them to define who we are.

I have a friend who struggles to overcome the deep, deep hurt caused by an abusive father. Her pain and simmering anger are entirely understandable. But my friend, now well into midlife, defines herself as the "child of an abusive father." That's her self-declared label, and no matter what happens in her life, everything always comes back to this painful reality. It has become the rationale for unhealthy habits and the explanation for unwise choices. She has accepted a new but false identity. She's allowing her father's abuse to define who she is. Overcoming the devastating effects of abuse is a monumental challenge. I hope for the day that my friend will be able to forgive her father, and in doing so, be freed to become the child of God she was always created to be.

The dying tend to take inventory of their lives simply because they are dying. Time may run out; important work remains to be done. In their reflection, many realize that hanging on to hurt makes no sense. They desire to live out their days in as much peace as possible. They do not want bitterness and resentment with them in their death bed. The dying see their world differently now that they know they are dying. They tend to be less judgmental and more understanding, and to realize that we have all made mistakes. In forgiving those who have hurt them, the dying actively choose to focus on the present and not be held captive by the past.

Here's the heart of the matter: we actually have a choice to make. We can choose to remain permanently wounded or we can choose to forgive, let go, and move on. This is not easy, but it is a choice. We can choose to be defined by our hurtful circumstances or we can choose, instead, to be defined by who we really are—beloved sons and daughters of our Heavenly Father.

EIGHTEEN

Sadness

M Y DYING FRIENDS TEACH ME THAT TEARS ARE A GIFT to be treasured. I was raised in an emotionally distant family. Although I knew I was loved and there was no question of my parents' desire to provide for me and care for me, words or actions that might signal some kind of emotion were rare. I was hard pressed to find a model for expressing love, joy, anger, sadness, disappointment, hope, grief. When Sharon, my wife-to-be, was introduced to my parents she had the audacity to hug them. That was very awkward for everyone. But to her credit, Sharon kept hugging, and eventually I began to hug them too. In time, they began to hug back.

The dying, through their tears, have taught me the nobility of crying. I used to think that emotional restraint was the more dignified course—do not make a fool of yourself and do not make others uncomfortable. Keep your feelings in check and your eyes dry—this is the superior path for those who can master it. I could not have been more wrong. Tears are necessary, healing, authentic, and more heroic than emotional suppression.

Most of my meetings with the dying involve tears—usually both theirs and mine. At times, the dying need to have some space, beyond the listening ears of family members, to release all their emotions without worrying about how their loved ones might be impacted. Although I do not try to make the dying cry, I have come to expect tears as entirely normal and helpful. Often, all it takes is one direct and sincere question while I look into their eyes and hold their gaze: How are you managing? How is your spouse coping? How are your children? How is it with your soul?

In his book *Our Greatest Gift*, Henri Nouwen introduces us to one of his co-workers and close friends, Connie, who is in the end stages of cancer. Connie, a grandmother, candidly shares her fears:

> "I am not afraid to die. I feel safe in God's love. I know that you and many others pray for me and that nothing bad can happen to me. But I worry about the kids." As she said this, she began to cry. "I don't want the kids to suffer because of me. I don't want them to become sad and sorrowful as they see me dying."[29]

It is liberating to get to that point where we can say, "I feel safe in God's love," and that "nothing bad can happen to me." The heart of Christian faith affirms that ultimately and eternally God holds us safe in his love. But the dying are intensely and understandably worried about their families.

Simon was dying and he knew it. Without a sudden and miraculous intervention from God, he would be dead within two years. About halfway through his season of dying, Simon began to cry, and there was absolutely nothing I could say or do to make things better, because they were not better. Simon was coming to grips with his imminent death. Medicine had failed him, and God, in his sovereignty, had chosen not to cure him. Soon he would be dead. Athletic, handsome, successful in business, with a strong faith, a great marriage, and two kids he adored, Simon would not see his fiftieth birthday.

I suggested to Simon that he might want to think about leaving some messages for his family—words of encouragement and expressions of love that they might be able to cherish after he was gone. I thought this might help Simon let go of that which he cared about the most. By the time Simon agreed, he was so weak he could not write or type, so we decided that a videotaped message might work best. This turned out to be much more traumatic than I ever envisioned. Whenever Simon started to think about what he might want to say to his wife and children, he began to cry uncontrollably. There was no fear in his tears—only the reality of loss in the here and now, the knowledge that he would not be here to love his family. He ached at the sorrow he would cause them by dying.

It took Simon months to wrap his head around the fact that he would not be there for his son and daughter to graduate from high school, to go to university, to date, to get married, to have children. He felt awful about leaving his wife to raise their children on her own. He knew that no danger lay ahead for him, that his future was certain, and that he would soon die into God's love. Yet, he experienced overwhelming sorrow that his family would have to carry on without him. As Simon struggled to leave his family behind, I would remind him that the same God who would soon receive him into eternity would also look after his family. Simon understood that, he really did. But surrendering his wife, son, and daughter still proved to be the hardest part of the journey.

Sadness over impending loss is normal and necessary. Our typical reaction to sad people is to cheer them up—to help them look at the bright side of life, at all the colorful and good things around them. But in doing this, we simply express our own inability to tolerate sadness. We are the ones who do not want to feel the sadness of the moment because it makes us uncomfortable, and, in the end, we want the sick person to feel better so that we feel better. We ask the sick person to alleviate our discomfort, to minister to us and make us feel better, to help us avoid feeling any real feelings, and to help protect us from seriously looking at ourselves. We ask the dying to shield us from our own dysfunction.

As the dying work through the process of accepting the impending loss of all that is precious and meaningful, attempts to cheer them up and reassure them all will be okay lack meaning.

> There is a time for everything, and a season for every
>   activity under the heavens:
> a time to weep and a time to laugh, a time to mourn
>   and a time to dance. . . .
> —Ecclesiastes 3:1, 4

> Like one who takes away a garment on a cold day,
> or like vinegar poured on soda, is one who sings songs
>   to a heavy heart.
> —Proverbs 25:20

If we encourage the dying to not be so sad, we get in the way of their coming to grips with losing everything and everyone they love. These days may be filled with silence and even withdrawal. We can bring life to our dying loved ones by entering into their suffering and sharing in their pain, but that can only happen when we stop denying our own pain, our own loss, our own grief and sadness. We do not make our pain the focus, but neither do we deny it. We cry together, sit in silence together, stare off into space together, and let them carry the conversation. We pray honest prayers with them. We ask God to help them in their sadness. We ask God for the courage to stay with them in their sadness.

As much as Simon trusted God and was not afraid to die, he exhibited overwhelming sadness at the thought of leaving the ones he loved. Sometimes Simon cried and cried—twenty, thirty, forty minutes at a time—not gentle crying but great, anguished sobbing that frightened me. I still see his contorted face and hear the unnatural sounds coming from deep inside him. I wondered at the time what I would do if he could not stop crying. Would he dissolve into a flood of tears? How could I give him back to his wife in this state?

I knew the tears were prompted by my questions, because I kept going to those hard places that no one else dared go. I asked him about what he still needed to say to his children before the disease left him without a voice. I asked him if he had talked to his wife about her life after he died—did he bless her to get remarried? I asked if he had accepted his death. On many days in Simon's season of tears, he was unable to respond to even one of my questions. No words—just uncontrollable, gut-wrenching sorrow flowing out of his eyes and his nose.

The best thing I did for Simon was simply let him cry—not demand anything of him, not insist he shape up, not preach at him. As the dying embrace their sadness, we can help by offering a safe place to cry, without the need to feel ashamed or explain their deep and convoluted emotions. As Simon's death approached, a deep peace and a quiet strength replaced his crying. He faced death with the quiet nobility and grace I hope to emulate one day.

NINETEEN

Dying Now

The real death—the passage from time into eternity, from
the transient beauty of this world to the lasting beauty of
the next, from darkness into light—has to be made now.

—HENRI NOUWEN[30]

VICKY IS ONE OF MY HEROES. WE WERE FRIENDS.
God gave me the privilege of helping Vicky die, and this she did at
the age of 58. We met regularly over the last five years of her life.
Mainly I just showed up and made myself available, and God did
the rest.

With a failed marriage behind her, and with two beautiful
daughters in tow, Vicky relocated to Oakville, found a job in
Toronto, and tried for a while to play the role of super mom.
Marriage had not worked for her, but she was determined not to
be a failure as a mom. And for a while, everything seemed to be
going well. But eight months after she moved to Oakville, chaos
ensued when she was diagnosed with breast cancer. Vicky was 37.
Treatment began: one year of chemo, two weeks on and two weeks
off. She got very sick, lost her hair, and was always tired. But she
recovered. Vicky said she felt she was back in control. She remembers
saying to herself, "I can beat this cancer! I just have to put a smile
on my face, have a positive attitude, and everything will be fine."

Four years later, chaos erupted once more. A lump showed
up in the scar tissue. More treatment followed: this time daily

radiation for six weeks. At the end, they sent Vicky home to wait and see. The following year, she began having trouble walking; the cancer had spread to her hip bone. She was given two years to live. A dozen years later, Vicky spoke about that time in her life to a group of women in our church:

> After the shock had worn off, I remember crying out to God and saying, "OK, you now have my full and complete attention," which I finally realized He had been trying to get all my life, especially over the past five years. But I had wanted to do things my way. I wanted to be in full control. How arrogant and full of pride I was. I finally understood, I was not in control and never had been. He was. I prayed to Him with abandonment and surrender, not for healing but that He would show me His will for the remainder of my life and that He would help me take care of my children. I also decided that I had to make the most of each day and live it to the fullest. In Isaiah 30:18, we read, "But the Lord still waits for you to come to him so He can show you his love and compassion. For the Lord is a faithful God." Jesus only wants us to say, "Not my will, but yours." That's all he had wanted. Why had I been so afraid? It was so simple.

The reason Vicky and so many others lived and died well is that they had already died to themselves and had opened up their hands to receive all that God desired to give them.

The death that comes at the end of every life will not be so fearful if we die well now, while we are still alive. Those who, like Vicky, have already died to themselves approach their physical death with a confident hope that all *is* well and all *will* be well. This hope is neither naïve nor trivial. As God has loved them in life, so he will love them in death and receive them as friends.

The ability to die well is made possible by having already died. I speak here of the most profound, life-altering, mind-blowing, paradigm-shifting experience that exists as a possibility for each one of us. This experience is characterized by submission to God and by death to self. It is a realization that we are not what we should be, we are not what we were made to be, and we are not what we could be. We realize and accept the love of the Creator God who desires so much more for us and who desires above all to be in loving relationship with us. We realize that there is an entire world out there, a physical world and a spiritual world, and if we are to embrace that world and be fully alive in that world, we need the help, love, and power of God, who created that world. We know we cannot do this on our own. God never intended for us to be on our own. It is *his* world that he invites us into . . . now and forever.

Jesus came to help us see that God's world is here and available for us to enter into, not when we die physically, but now. As our hearts and minds and spirits submit to God, we have the opportunity to truly live. As we surrender and submit to the Higher Power, the Higher Love, the Higher Wisdom, the Higher Truth, we will be more alive than we ever thought possible. Is that easy? Of course not. Surrender and submission go against our nature. Will it be safe? Absolutely not. To be fully alive is never safe. That is why so many of us fail to experience full life.

"I have come that they may have life, and have it to the full."
—Jesus, in John 10:10

Beyond his group of 12 disciples, Jesus had other dear friends. He was particularly close to Lazarus and his sisters, Mary and Martha. Tragically, in the Gospel story Lazarus dies while Jesus is off travelling. He returns to the grieving sisters, both of whom tell Jesus that Lazarus would not have died if Jesus had been present. I'm not sure if these are statements of faith or accusations of blame. Jesus is deeply moved at their grief and at the death of one he loved. The apostle John simply tells us, "Jesus wept." Jesus understands what it means for us to grieve.

But Jesus does something curious in the midst of his conversation with Mary and Martha. He takes the focus off their brother's physical death and begins to talk about life. He reorients the death-event and turns it into a life-event. Jesus says to Martha,

> "Your brother will rise again. . . . I am the resurrection
> and the life. The one who believes in me will live, even
> though they die; and whoever lives by believing in me
> will never die. Do you believe this?"
> —John 11:23-26

Jesus chooses not to dwell on the death, but on the truth that there is something greater at play here. Something more powerful and more important is taking place. Jesus wants Martha to see this. He asks her, "Do you believe this?" I think Jesus is saying, "Do you understand what I'm talking about. Do you get it? This is not the end. Lazarus has already accomplished the first and most important death because he has believed in me. And so, this second death, as painful as it is to us, will not keep Lazarus in the grave. He will never die because he has died already."

Martha responds with the declaration:

"Yes, Lord, I believe that you are the Christ, the Son of God."

Martha gets it.

We need Christ to help us die now. We need Christ to help us love well now. We need Christ to help us live well now. Then, we will be prepared to die well later.

Shortly after he turned forty, a friend of mine said the most important thing left for him to do was to die well. Wow! He was 40, not 80. But I think he might be on to something. This was no morbid thought on his part but a deeply reflective response that would, if pursued, affect how he lived out the rest of his days.

Although the ALS slowly destroyed every muscle in his body, Dave made peace with his fatal disease. He believed he was in God's hands no matter the outcome. His faith in God kept trumping any desire for a cure. When the subject of fear or what the future might hold came up, Dave often said with a mischievous grin, "God is still on the throne and he ain't nervous!" Dave could not conceive of God anxiously wringing his hands, worried about what the future might hold. His declaration that God sat fearlessly on his throne rang out as a battle cry and a declaration of ultimate submission, of allowing God to be God. Dave acknowledged that God knew his current condition, and that God's ultimate plan for humanity was not in jeopardy just because Dave was dying. Dave knew God loved him, and when he died, God would still love him. God was not nervous about Dave's death and neither was Dave. Dave had already died to self.

TWENTY

Overcoming Fear

Why is it that the only time we contemplate the soul in an everlasting way is when someone else dies, when we are standing at an open grave, wondering why we can't find the right words to speak to one another? Is it because all we can think of is our own impending doom? Is it fear that keeps our contemplative selves quiet? Is it fear of the question: when that little spark of energy leaves our bodies does that little spark go to heaven? Or is it fear of the even simpler question: does it go anywhere?

—DAVID CROWDER AND MIKE HOGAN[31]

ALTHOUGH I DIDN'T KNOW HER, I DISTINCTLY REMEMBER when my grandmother died. She lived in Germany and I lived in British Columbia with my mom, dad, sister, and two brothers. I was four or five years old at the time. The picture I have in my head is of my father sitting quietly alone in a chair in our living room. I went into the room to ask him something. I cannot remember what it was, but I know he didn't answer. What I do remember, quite clearly, is my mother quickly ushering me out of the room and telling me to leave my father alone. She told me he had just received word from Germany that his mother had died. My dad sat there, alone, for a very long time. I was not sure what to think or do, and so I stayed away from Dad for the rest of the day. I do not recall another word ever being spoken about my grandmother's death.

The next day, everything seemed normal.

When I was seven I saw a cat die. It was the most frightening experience of my young life. It was summertime and I was playing outdoors with my siblings. I saw our neighbor's black cat in our front yard and went to play with it. The cat ran under a car that was parked directly in front of our house. I could see it hiding under the car. I slowly walked over to the car, got down on my hands and knees and reached out for the cat. I wanted the cat to come to me so I could play with it. Instead, the frightened cat ran out from under the car onto the road. I saw everything as I looked under the car. A car hit the cat with its front driver side tire. The tire ran right over the cat. The cat rolled over several times from the force of the blow. The car never stopped, and all that was left was a half-dead cat in the middle of the road. Somehow the cat dragged itself to the opposite curb where it laid down and died. I knew it was dead. I saw it all. I ran to the back yard of our house and hid. I was terrified. It felt like it was my fault. I only wanted to play with the cat. What if our neighbors found out what had happened? Fear and guilt overwhelmed me. I felt so bad for the cat and for the little girl who owned the cat.

After a few days, life got back to normal. I never told anyone what happened.

When I was 15, I hung out with a group of guys who would get together weekly for parties, poker, movies, and sports. One Saturday morning about 10 AM, there was a knock on my bedroom door. The knock woke me up. I mumbled some kind of acknowledgment and the door opened to reveal two of my best friends. I knew something was wrong—my friends never came knocking on a Saturday morning. I remember lying there, still in bed, seeing these two guys silhouetted in the door of my bedroom, and one of them said, "We've got bad news." And they proceeded to tell me that one of our friends had been driving home the previous night and had been hit head-on by a drunk driver. The drunk driver survived. Our friend did not. They told me the news, stayed a few minutes, and left. It felt like a bad dream. I could not wrap my head around what I had just heard. It did not make sense. I felt numb. Over the next few days I just did not know what to do. I couldn't bear to face our dead friend's family. I did not know if I should send a card. What would I say? So, I did nothing—I didn't even go to the funeral. I was too afraid. I had never been to a funeral. My mind and my emotions seemed quite incapable of processing what had taken place. It just didn't make sense. He was dead. What did that even mean?

A few weeks later, life returned to normal. I never talked to anyone about my friend's death.

We have an inbred fear of death. Deep down, we know that no matter how strong our belief in a loving God, death is still the big unknown. Alan Segal, in his book *Life After Death*, puts it this way, "Death anxiety infects everything we do as humans, even when we are trying to be brave. It is part of the human condition; indeed it seems a consequence of self-consciousness itself. It is a price we pay for being aware of ourselves as beings."[32]

Every time we think about death more than casually, every time we attend a funeral, every time we look into a casket, every time we stand at the edge of a grave as the body is lowered, we face our mortality and our fear. With an unsettling disquiet in our gut, a sadness in our hearts, and a lot of confusion in our minds, we fear the end of our life.

Throughout human history, one question haunts us: What happens after we die?

I am not sure what frightens us more: to consider that after death there is nothingness, complete nonexistence—or to consider that we might encounter the God of the Universe who is all powerful and knows absolutely everything about us.

Douglas Coupland's greatest fear is that God exists but does not care very much for humans.[33] I suspect that Coupland's fear is much more personal. He is afraid that God might not like *him*.

To suggest that somehow my dead and dying friends were immune from fear would be a horrible lie. There are many fears that the sick and dying have:

They fear suffering.

They fear losing their ability to look after themselves.

They are afraid they will not have the courage to face death.

They fear not being able to cope with all the things they need to do and say before they die.

They are afraid of how their loved ones will react if they express all of their fears out loud.

They are afraid of what their fear of death says about their faith.

They are afraid of what their fear of death says about who they are.

They are just plain afraid of the unknown.

Most of our fears have to do with death or the possibility of death. Death is the ultimate fear that we face as human beings. And therein lies the gift to the dying and their loved ones. They are forced to face their ultimate fear, and in that encounter comes the possibility of being released not only from their greatest fear but all the other lesser fears that keep them from living. They stop worrying about all the things that have not happened and learn to live in the present with the things that are happening. The dying learn that many of their fears are not based in reality. Death, however, is real.

The dying have no choice but to face the ultimate fear of death. And as they face that fear they begin to realize that it does not crush them, and, in fact, it ceases to have power over them. The power lies in the fear itself and not in the actual death. Death is real and cannot be overcome. Fear is real and can be overcome.

Many of us spend enormous amounts of time and energy worrying about things that never happen. Insurance companies have built a multi-billion-dollar industry based on our fears and based on the high probability that those fears will not materialize. Fear takes away our freedom and gives society the power to manipulate us with threats and promises. It keeps us from experiencing joy, peace, contentment, happiness, and fulfillment. Fear limits the potential God intended for us. It keeps us from intimate relationships and significant commitments.

Speaking in public is often cited as one of our classic fears. What if I forget what I'm supposed to say? What if the words don't come out right? What if I trip going up to the front? What if they don't like what I have to say? I'm not good enough to be up there. They will see right through me. They will know I'm afraid and weak and don't know what I'm doing.

Lorie hid behind Dave most of her married life. Lorie's insecurity and many fears resulted in Dave's becoming the public front for the two of them. Whether they were at a social function or a business affair, or in their faith community, Dave did most of the talking. Shortly after the doctors diagnosed Dave's ALS, Dave and Lorie started attending the small group that my wife and I ran. Lorie said very little in the group. She seemed quite timid, even fearful, unsure of herself. And she never ever prayed out loud. We were all aware of what Dave and Lorie were going through, and we prayed with them and for them every week. Dave entered into those prayer times in meaningful ways. Lorie never did. She said she couldn't—she was too afraid.

But something powerful was at work in Lorie. Death compelled her to overcome her fears. As Lorie faced Dave's declining health, she did so with increasing vitality and force. She attended to his every need, fighting the disease every step of the way. She knew the prognosis, but the closer Dave got to the end, the stronger and more confident Lorie became. Dave was no longer able to speak or pray for the two of them. During the three-and-a-half-year battle with ALS, Lorie overcame her fears of speaking and praying in public. She became a powerful advocate for Dave and a dynamic witness to God's strength and faithfulness in desperate times.

Lorie looked death in the face for nearly four years and, in the end, there was little else to be afraid of. Lorie was devastated by the loss of her young husband but, now, there are many things that Lorie does that she never would have thought possible while Dave was alive and healthy.

So much is possible when fear no longer holds us captive. If I could reach into you and remove all your fears—every one of them—how different would your life be? Imagine a world without fear. If nothing stopped you from following your dreams and living the life you always wanted to live, how would your life change? These are the questions that my dying friends have prompted in me as I watch them face the worst of all fears and, in the process, see the rest of their fears taken away.

My dying friends have taught me that getting beyond my fears requires the embrace of love. It really is God's perfect love that drives out fear. As the dying recognize and receive the love of God and the love of others, they overcome fear's debilitating effect. *Believing* they are loved and *feeling* they are loved allows them to get beyond being afraid. The dying who have overcome their fears understand what God has been telling us all along: he loves us. And if the God of the universe loves us, we do not need to be afraid. If the most powerful Being in existence is for us, we do not need to worry.

God's consistent message to us through his Word is that we should not be afraid. Why? Because he loves us. This is incredibly simple. And powerful.

Over and over again, God says to us, "Do not be afraid." "Fear not." "Don't worry." "Don't be anxious." And over and over again, God affirms his love for us. It is no accident that these are two of the most dominant themes in all of Scripture. Although I have been involved in pastoral counseling for many years, I am not a psychologist, psychiatrist, or philosopher. But my experience and my instincts tell me that there are likely two core choices at work in our lives: fear and love. Living in fear produces negative and harmful feelings such as rejection, low self-esteem, anger, hate, jealousy, and guilt. Fear binds us and constricts our focus to ourselves. If you dig deep enough, there is an underlying fear behind all of these negative feelings. Choosing a life of love results in positive and healthy emotions such as hope, peace, joy, contentment, trust, and self-confidence. Love frees us and enlarges our focus to others. Love moves us beyond our self-centeredness.

God is love. Whoever lives in love lives in God and
God in them. This is how love is made complete
among us so that we will have confidence on the day of
judgment: In this world we are like Jesus. There is no
fear in love. But perfect love drives out fear, because
fear has to do with punishment. The one who fears
is not made perfect in love. We love because he first
loved us.
—1 John 4:16-19

For I am convinced that neither death nor life, neither
angels nor demons, neither the present nor the future,
nor any powers, neither height nor depth, nor anything
else in all creation, will be able to separate us from the
love of God that is in Christ Jesus our Lord.
—Romans 8:38-39

God knows that we fear death, and he went to extreme lengths
to help us overcome that fear. Jesus, the very Son of God, came
into this world as one of us, a fully human being. At the end of
his life, Jesus overcame death—for us. He defeated death—for us.
Death is not a hole we fall into, never to emerge. Jesus made death
a passageway to new life. He proved death was not the end and
promised us eternal life with him. In Jesus's death on the cross
and in his resurrection three days later, Jesus says to us: "You
do not need to be afraid of death anymore. I've taken care of it—
because I love you."

A number of years ago, Amy, a wife and the mother of four young children, was hospitalized with a life-threatening infection. One night, when the infection was at its worst, Amy felt that she was dying. In reality, she was very close to death. She was worried and overwhelmed and did not want to let go of her husband and children. During that night, Amy had an encounter with Jesus. She had a vision that she was walking through the valley of the shadow of death and heading towards heaven. She remembers being able to see heaven off in the distance. In her vision, Jesus came along and picked her up and began to carry her. At first she was still frightened, but then her fear melted away. She realized that she was okay and things would be okay even if she had to leave her family.

Amy understood that being in the presence of Jesus made her fear go away. Up until this point in life, she would never talk about death and was even uncomfortable with the topic of heaven because it meant an end to the life she loved here on earth. But in Jesus's presence, she no longer had to cling to her family or her life. In the vision, she came to a place of total peace. That was when she realized Jesus was no longer carrying her towards heaven but back towards her hospital bed. Her peace came not from her physical healing but from his presence. Ever since that night, Amy says she no longer fears death because she knows that ultimately she and her family will be okay no matter what. She is quick to point out that this lack of fear is not indifference but rather a supernatural assurance.

TWENTY-ONE

Ignoring Death

In Victorian times, neighbors and friends would gather
around a person who was approaching the gates of death.
They would listen to any words of wisdom that might fall
from cracked and swollen lips, contribute what strength
they could through prayers and hymns, and try to learn
from what they believed to be the most significant moment
of life for a Christian.

—PHILIP YANCEY[34]

ON THIS PARTICULAR MORNING, BREAKFAST WITH MY FRIEND
Ross took about two-and-a-half hours instead of our regular sixty
minutes. After talking about our children and parents and siblings
and matters of faith, Ross asked what I was planning to do for the
rest of my sabbatical. And so we started talking about the death
and dying book I was writing.

We discussed the difficulty people have in talking to a dying
person about their death. And that people find it very hard to have
a conversation with someone whose loved one is dying. Often,
they say silly, meaningless, inappropriate, and sometimes even
hurtful things.

I told Ross what many people say and do in these circumstances
is really an attempt to make themselves feel better. In order to
avoid connecting with the pain, grief, and sadness, they say things
that reassure themselves that everything is okay.

Ross and Wendy have two children. A third child, Leah, was stillborn. As we talked, Ross recounted some of the events and feelings around those days of profound grief and sorrow. About two months after they buried their daughter, a business colleague came to see him. This was the first time they had met since Leah's death. He came into Ross's office without saying a word, hugged him, and cried with him. Without words, without Scripture, without prayer, there was more comfort and connection in that hug and in those tears than in many of the attempts by Ross's closer and more religious friends who tried to comfort him with empty words.

Ross remembered with surprising emotion the people who avoided him and refused to say anything. He said, "I can understand people tripping over themselves trying to say the right thing and not knowing what to say and even saying some dumb things, but what I can't understand are the people who deliberately avoided me."

We treat death as a stranger—a stranger to be avoided and not to be talked to. In fact, it is better that we do not even look at the stranger, lest he look back at us. We have great difficulty contemplating and accepting the fact that we will die. Some have even suggested it is psychologically impossible to fully come to grips with one's own death. We have a strong inherent belief in our own immortality.

The unpleasantness of death, the trauma to our psyche when we try to think about death, and the fear of the great unknowns of death move us to a state of avoiding death at all costs. We do not want to look at it. We do not want to talk about it, at least not in any serious way. We objectify what we're afraid of: we put it on TV and watch it over and over again until it no longer has any effect on us. The deaths of other people in other places are okay to talk about. It's okay to feel a certain amount of genuine empathy and concern for those who have lost their lives and those who are left behind. But the whole time we are feeling empathy, we are also thinking, "That's not me—I'm still alive."

It is so very hard to look at our own death or the death of someone close to us. Our mind shuts down. Our heart cannot seem to go there. It is too sad and scary, so we retreat and ignore, we suppress and avoid.

> Ivan Ilyich saw that he was dying, and he was in perpetual despair.
>
> In the depths of his heart, he knew he was dying, but not only was he not accustomed to the thought, he simply did not and could not grasp it.
>
> "If I had to die . . . I should have known it was so. An inner voice would have told me so, but there was nothing of the sort in me. . . . It can't be. It's impossible! But here it is. How is this? How is one to understand it?"
>
> He could not understand it, and tried to drive this false, incorrect, morbid thought away and to replace it by other proper and healthy thoughts.
>
> —Leo Tolstoy[35]

Ignoring death is worse than being afraid of death. At least with fear, we are still engaged in some way. We are still thinking about death or looking at death. When we ignore death we completely disengage. We pretend that death does not exist.

Since the two world wars of the past century, we have worked hard at sanitizing death. We isolate death to critical care wards, emergency rooms, and chronic care facilities where it remains hidden from view.

In spite of looking upon death every day, we rarely engage with death. Numbed by news, TV, movies, and video games, we see death as an event that occurs on a screen where it is safely unreal. It may occur in other countries and in other neighborhoods but not here, not where we live, not to us. Death cannot touch us or so we think.

Talking about death "over there," whether it be in Darfur, or Malawi, or India is seen as socially acceptable and even admirable. We are human and we care about the poor, the refugees, and the victims of injustice and disaster. But talking about my death or your death or the death of a loved one is different. That's uncomfortable, maybe even morbid, and certainly socially inappropriate.

Quite logically, ignoring death causes us to be ignorant about death. We do not even know how to have a decent conversation about what is arguably one of the most important events of our lives. We shy away from the dying, not knowing what to say or what to do or where to look. We do not know how to feel or what to hope for. We do not know how to pray. Do we pray for healing or a quick and painless death? Do we ask God to take them soon or let them stay? Do we tell them they look good?—How does that sound to a dying woman? Do we engage in small talk? Will they care about the weather forecast? Or whether the local sports team won or lost? Or whether the stock exchange was up or down? What if they start to cry? What if I start to cry?

But in desperately trying to avoid death, we end up ignoring the people who are dying and, in doing so, we miss out on their deep wisdom and profound insights. We miss out on learning what it means to truly be alive. We miss out on the life-giving work of reflecting on our own impending death. We fail to sort out what is authentically important and what is just cosmetically pleasing to the senses—what's going to last and what's going to wash off by bedtime.

TWENTY-TWO

Ars Moriendi

THERE IS A BODY OF HISTORICAL CHRISTIAN LITERATURE dating back to the 1400s known as *Ars Moriendi,* or the "art of dying." These books and manuals provided practical guidance for the dying and their caregivers. They were intended to help people die a good death.

An English translation appeared around 1450 under the title *The Book of the Craft of Dying.* The first chapter praises the deaths of good Christians and repentant sinners who die "gladly and wilfully" in God.[36] Because the best preparation for a good death is a good life, Christians should "live in such wise . . . that they may die safely, every hour, when God will."[37] What followed the two original versions of the *Ars Moriendi* was a lengthy tradition of Christian works on preparation for death. But nearly all subsequent authors placed the "art of dying" within a broader "art of living," which itself required a consistent *memento mori,* or awareness of and preparation for one's own death.[38] That is the challenge and call of the dying to the living. That is the heart of God for each one of us. His Son, Jesus, came so that we might have abundant life, life to the full, life to the max. As we master the art of living in its fullest and most complete God-infused possibilities, we will be prepared for a good and life-giving death.

Andrew and I have been pastoral colleagues and friends for many years. In his late 30s, with a wife and four sons, Andrew entered a prolonged season of dying that was frustrating, confusing, alarming, and increasingly debilitating.

For a couple of years, Andrew's health declined gradually without any hint of a diagnosis. It began with weakness, anxiety, weight gain, high blood pressure, and high blood sugar. In the second year of his illness, the decline picked up speed and became a runaway train with little hope of a good outcome. Andrew began experiencing chills, sleeplessness, swelling, digestion and bladder issues, kidney and liver problems—and the list kept growing. Doctors did multiple scans, ultrasounds, and MRIs, and countless blood and urine tests. It appeared that every system in Andrew's body was misfiring or shutting down.

Eventually the doctors confirmed that Andrew was suffering from Cushing's Disease. With this disease, a small tumor forms on the pituitary gland, essentially causing it to go to sleep. A healthy pituitary gland regulates the hormone levels in the body, but with Cushing's, the production of hormones is unchecked—like a valve stuck in the open position. Andrew had 7000 times the normal level of cortisol in his body, and he was beginning to shut down. The only treatment for Cushing's is neurosurgery—up through the nose and dangerously close to the brain. By the time Andrew got to surgery, he was so sick that doctors estimated he had only a few weeks to live. Surgery was successful in terms of removing the tumor, but Andrew's post-operative condition was not one of recovery but of further, dramatic decline. Andrew began to have major difficulty breathing, and it appeared to everyone, including

Andrew, that he was in the final hours of his life. The doctors ran more tests and discovered a pulmonary embolism, a saddle clot, had formed in the artery between his heart and lungs. His situation was critical. The next morning, Andrew was barely conscious and struggling to breathe. Doctors were unsure of how to proceed. They could not treat the clot with blood thinners because of the high risk he would bleed to death from his surgical site. They did not feel Andrew was strong enough to survive open heart surgery to remove the clot. Andrew vaguely recalls the tension and raised voices as three doctors discussed and argued about how to proceed as they gathered around his critical care bed. They were, however, agreed on one thing—if they did nothing, Andrew would certainly die. In the end, they treated the clot by inserting a catheter through his leg up to the site of the clot. Their plan was to release some blood thinner locally and hope for the best. But, as one of the doctors feared, Andrew's surgical site began to bleed. Blood began to pour out of his nose. They were forced to stop treatment and worked to stem the bleeding. It was now a matter of wait and see. That night, Andrew fully anticipated he would die and worked hard to prepare for death by surrendering and releasing. He took hold of the promise that God loved his family and friends more than he did and he could entrust those he loved to God. That night Andrew's family and friends gathered to pray. The next morning, he was still alive. Andrew remained in hospital for three weeks, recovering from neurosurgery, from his close brush with death, and from years of being flooded with cortisol. Five months later, Andrew is still recovering but is feeling better than he has in many years.

On his first Sunday back in church, Andrew was asked to reflect on the final year leading up to the eventual diagnosis and surgery. During this time, the doctors and Andrew knew there was something seriously wrong. How did Andrew deal with the uncertainty he was facing? How did he prepare for whatever might be coming?

Andrew's short answer was that he became quite intentional about living well. He faced the very real possibility he was in his last months or years and began working through an inventory of his life. He started by looking at his relationships and honestly assessing whether there was anyone he needed to forgive. Was there any unfinished business to deal with? Andrew understood that for his own sake, he needed to forgive those people who had hurt or offended him. He had no desire to carry any lasting hurt or bitterness into an uncertain future.

Then Andrew asked God to bring to his mind all those people from whom he needed to seek forgiveness—anyone he had hurt or offended by his actions or words. He made a list and started contacting people, confessing his wrongdoings, asking for forgiveness and offering to make things right. Although this was harder than forgiving others, Andrew discovered most people were amazingly gracious when he came clean with them.

The third thing Andrew did was thank people who had been a blessing or an encouragement to him over the years. Each month he would contact one person—an old college roommate, a lady who used to babysit him, a friend from childhood, members of his own family, people from church, people he played hockey with—and thanked them and told them how God had used them in his life. He did not tell them he was sick, he just thanked them. Andrew acknowledged it was a little weird calling up someone out of the blue, some after 20 years, to tell them you appreciate them and want to buy them lunch. They think you are dying or need money or perhaps are having marriage problems. People do not always get it when you say, "I just want to bless you." But in the end, they all appreciated Andrew's words, and Andrew felt good every time he took the opportunity to express gratitude. Andrew was living well in order to die well.

Andrew asked the elders of the church to come and pray over him and anoint him with oil for healing. He began letting go of his pastoral responsibilities, entrusting them into the care and safekeeping of his younger colleagues. He put his finances in order. He fixed things around the house to make it easier for his family. Andrew wrote letters to each one of his boys and to his dear wife, letters of affirmation and blessing and love and delight. They all still have their letters.

During the two days following surgery, with his life hanging in the balance, Andrew had a profound encounter with Christ. In his mind, Andrew was back on the family farm of his childhood. As he was walking along the back lane, he heard a voice from behind him ask, "Will you give me today?" Andrew knew this was a question about surrender. God was asking him to surrender today as if it were the last day of his life. Andrew understood this surrender was to include everything that particular day held for his health, his family, his wife, his kids—it was about giving everything to God. It was hard for Andrew to surrender so completely because he knew if he gave God his life, God might simply say "Thank you" and take it.

Andrew surrendered and thought his encounter was over, but then he heard another question, "Will you give me tomorrow?" And by *tomorrow* God meant all his tomorrows, the things he was looking forward to, his dreams and hopes. Again, Andrew found it difficult to fully surrender, knowing that he might never experience tomorrow—but he did. Having given God today and tomorrow, Andrew again thought he had finished—but he heard one more question: "Will you give me yesterday?" And Andrew thought, I will gladly give you all the days of my illness; but then God clarified, "Will you give me yesterday with thanksgiving?"

The next day Andrew did a simple exercise of giving God those three days again—today, tomorrow, and yesterday. He started by giving God the new day and all he was currently facing and all the people he would encounter. Then he picked a future day he still wanted to experience, and finally he gave God a day in the past he was thankful for.

Andrew is becoming better at giving God his todays, tomorrows, and yesterdays. He admits he is not at the point of thanking God for letting him get deathly sick, although he acknowledges God is bringing good out of it.

Andrew began to live better when confronted with the real possibility he would die. In living better, he was preparing for a good death. God says we do not know when we will die, so we ought to live in such a way that we are ready to die on any given day. This is to be our regular approach to life, not something out of the ordinary, but our normal state of being. Yet, most of the time, we live as if there is no end in sight. We tell ourselves that we will deal with our fractured relationships tomorrow, but tomorrow never comes.

I often hear people talk about what they plan to do differently when they get to retirement age, and their list of activities sounds more noble, spiritual, and meaningful than what they are doing right now. They talk about working for 16 hours a day for the first 30 years, establishing their security, putting away savings, getting the house and cottage paid off, and making sure they can afford to live out their final years in relative comfort. Then, upon retirement, they will focus more on helping the poor, giving back to society, volunteering in the church, spending more time with family, and generally making the world a better place.

What would these people do if they knew they had 24 months to live?

Ignoring death distorts our priorities and keeps us from living and loving the way God intended. Ignoring death keeps us from knowing God. Little in life brings us to God's doorstep more attentively than an encounter with death. Without the crisis of death, our spirituality tends to float along, not tried and tested, not deep, not intimate.

God says, "Try me, test me, taste me. . . ."

Some time ago, I was introduced to the concept of a good death being a "forward" death. I cannot remember where I was or who said it, but the idea was proposed in the context of a discussion on the life of a church. The speaker suggested that for a church to shut down and close its doors was not in itself a tragedy. In fact, it might be cause for celebration if the death of that church was a forward death. If the church, in dying, were able to advance God's kingdom, it would be a forward and good death. If the church were able to give life to other churches, it would be a forward and good death. If the church were able to uphold righteousness and truth, it would be a forward and good death.

The death of Martin Luther King Jr. was a forward, life-giving death. His death embodied the kingdom qualities of standing up for the oppressed and caring for the poor. His violent death was a peace-filled, noble fight against immoral laws and attitudes. Life continues to flow from his death to this day. Enormous good has come from King's life *and death*.

If a man, woman, or child dies so that love, truth, and justice are upheld, theirs is a forward death, advancing God's kingdom and giving life to others. If death brings peace, forgiveness, and hope, it is a forward death to be celebrated. If one dies in a way that points to God, it is a forward death that advances the kingdom and brings life for eternity.

TWENTY-THREE

Surprising Life

THERE IS A FASCINATING AND UNDENIABLE SERIES OF connections between life, love, and death. It is not the kind of connection that can be charted on a graph or described by a polynomial equation. It is not a direct correlation that allows us to predict what will happen if we tweak one of the variables. These connections are delicate and intricate. They are a bit unpredictable and at times appear frustratingly random. They defy the kind of logic used by mathematicians and statisticians and research scientists. The connections also seem to defy common sense. Many of the dying would say they have never felt more alive. Death, for them, has brought an increased intensity to life and love. Some of the dying would say that they would not change their condition. Knowing what they know now, they would not go back to life before encountering death. Death has brought meaning to their lives. Death has brought resolution to the question of God's existence. Death has brought a deeper communion with family and friends.

If we do not ignore death and move beyond our fear of death, we find that in many ways, death becomes a source for new life.

When people face their own death or experience the death of a loved one, there is a real possibility that new life will emerge in them and in those around them. This does not always happen. Not everyone is open to this new life. Not everyone is able to get beyond the fear and the pain and the tragic circumstances. But many have experienced this new life. I have seen it in my friends as we have walked together in their season of dying. And I have been the recipient of this new life on occasion: the dying have given me new life.

I know what I have observed and felt is not unique to me or my circle of friends. People such as Henri Nouwen, C. S. Lewis, Peter Kreeft, Leo Tolstoy, Annie Dillard, Douglas Coupland, Frederick Buechner—the list could go on and on—all have given voice in some way to the same belief. Where there is death, new life is possible.

And without a doubt, this is true because Jesus told us it is true. Jesus told his disciples (in John 14) that he was going to die, and that when he died, things would get better. Try telling that to your loved ones. This was a shocking statement. The disciples did not understand what Jesus was telling them, but they understood it later, and so do we. Out of Jesus's death comes the possibility for all of humanity to receive new life.

Jesus speaks with incredible candor about his death. We have much to learn from him. Jesus knew his death would bring sorrow and sadness, but he also affirmed over and over that his death was a good thing, full of promise and full of life.

Now I am going to him who sent me. None of you asks me, "Where are you going?" Rather, you are filled with grief because I have said these things. But very truly I tell you, *it is for your good that I am going away.* Unless I go away, the Advocate will not come to you; but if I go, I will send him to you.

I have much more to say to you, more than you can now bear. But when he, the Spirit of truth, comes, he will guide you into all truth. He will not speak on his own; he will speak only what he hears, and he will tell you what is yet to come.

—John 16: 5-7, 12-13, emphasis added

When he died, Jesus sent the Holy Spirit to the disciples. He claimed his connection with the disciples would get stronger, not weaker, after his death. Even though he would be physically absent from them, through his Spirit he would be more intimately connected with them than ever. He told them they would believe and understand things that before his death did not make sense. When Jesus walked this earth, he was in close and intimate relationship with only a small group of people. With the sending of his Spirit, Jesus is now able to be in intimate connection with every human being at the same time. This is an incredible gift that came from his death.

Too often, we think of the words and ways of Jesus as being beyond human possibility. We think, "that was Jesus," so those things don't apply to us. But the words and ways of Jesus, including his death, are intended to be our model, our example of how to live life fully and die well. What if Jesus's words about his death were to become our words about our death? Could we dare say to our loved ones and our friends, "It is for your own good that I am going, because if I go, there will come new truth, new hope, new life. My death will be a gift of life for you. The Spirit will come to you and reveal to you the things that are yet to come."[39]

I must confess that I do not fully grasp this thought. It seems strange and foreign, and yet this is the way of Jesus who said, "Very truly I tell you, unless a kernel of wheat falls into the earth and dies, it remains only a single seed; but if it dies, it produces many seeds" (John 12:24). And what is this rich harvest, this fruitfulness that continues beyond the grave? Will it be achieving the fourth-quarter targets for your company? Will it be that dream house you settle into upon retirement? Will it be the sum total of your financial estate? Will it be the race you won in the second year of college? Will it be the educational degrees you have accumulated over the years? When we begin to think about a harvest lasting beyond the grave, none of these things seem to matter anymore.

Henri Nouwen asks a haunting question: Will our death give new life, new hope, and new faith to our friends, or will it be no more than another cause for sadness?[40] Even thinking about this question, let alone attempting a response, requires a paradigm shift in how I perceive my life. It moves me from obsessing over how much I can still accomplish in the years I have left, to living in such a way that my dying will be a new way to send God's Spirit to those whom I love and who love me. What I am talking about here is the core biblical concept that death actually produces new life. That was true of Jesus's death, and it should be true of every one of our deaths. As Christians, we are to give new life and new hope and new faith to those around us, right? That's our mission in life. But it is also our mission in death. If we live well and die well, new life and new hope and new faith will continue to manifest in others even after we die.

Death is surprising in many ways. The most surprising dimension of death is new life. Life is not what you expect at all. When you look into the face of death you expect a black hole, emptiness, loss, sorrow, grief, separation. And while all of these are true to some extent, what is truly surprising is to find new life. New life always surprises us and fills us with hope and joy.

Every newborn baby surprises me. New life! How incredible! What joy and hope for the future. Even more surprising is to discover new life in the midst of death and dying. I remember the collapse of the twin towers in New York and how the falling towers had created a field of death—a massive graveyard for nearly 3000 men and women. I remember the surprise, the shock, and the renewed hope when two policemen were discovered alive under the rubble 24 hours after the buildings had imploded. We don't expect to see images of life in fields of death, but it happens all the time.

This is one of my favorite images. The fact that I started out as a forester probably has something to do with it. I love the picture of new life emerging out of old, dead stumps. Every time I see this, I am surprised and filled with hope. Foresters know the value of dead things—dead trees, old stumps, rotten logs, decomposing leaves. These are incubators for new life.

Foresters also understand the need for fires. The jack pine forests of northern Canada would die off if not for the deadly and rejuvenating forest fires. It is only with intense heat that the pine cones open up and release a new generation of seeds. And the seeds need the preparation of the scorching fires to find suitable places to germinate. The fires clear the brush, the leaves, and shrubs, preparing the ground to receive new life. In fact, if the fire (that is, death) does not come, life for the jack pine will cease.

TWENTY-FOUR

Bob's Story

For nearly 12 years, Bob and I met almost weekly. Over the years, we formed a close friendship built on prayer, kingdom mission, vulnerability, respect, tears, and fun. He was in many ways a remarkable man and a true friend. Before going any further, I simply want to state that Bob's death is a good death. It gives me no joy to say that—I would much rather Bob were still alive—but proclaiming Bob's death as a good death gives me some comfort. In living and dying the way he did, the kingdom of God is advancing. In living and dying the way he did, Bob continues to give life to me. In living and in dying the way he did, Bob is like a directional sign that keeps pointing me to God.

Luci Shaw tells of a refrigerator magnet that she received from a friend with the words "Live Generatively." For Shaw, this was an encouragement to take risks, to be a "universe-disturber for good," to move in a life-giving direction for the sake of others, and to contribute to the energy of the world.[41] This kind of living results in a forward death, a death that will continue to bring light into dark places, a death that will advance good and diminish evil, a death that will spread love and erode hate. Bob was a universe-disturber for good.

One of the remarkable things about Bob is that he did not understand why we considered him remarkable. In the years that followed the death of his two children, what we considered so unusual about his steadfastness, faithfulness, and lack of bitterness, Bob simply did not get. When people asked him to speak about his experiences of profound loss, he politely declined every time, suggesting he had nothing significant to say. Partly, Bob did not want to draw attention to himself, but mainly he felt he was only living out his faith in Christ and there was nothing remarkable about doing what was expected of every believer. I remember having several conversations with him about this very topic, trying to convince him that his response to tragic circumstances, and, even apart from those circumstances, the way he was living his life, was quite remarkable—and he really did having something to share with the rest of us. Bob, on the other hand, believed he was simply being obedient to Scripture. And, of course, Bob was right. He was, in fact, living out what is expected of any follower of Jesus—to live faithfully in the good times and the bad times. What made Bob remarkable is he actually did that.

> Shall we accept good from God, and not trouble?
> —Job 2:10

Bob was very successful in the eyes of this world, and yet he was incredibly humble. Bob was even more successful in the ways of the kingdom, and one of the marks of success in the kingdom is humility. As we said our good-byes to Bob on the night before he died, the word that Leslie used to describe her husband was *humble*. When the person who knows Bob the best and sees him at his worst describes him as humble, you know it's true. For Bob, humility was not an act, it was a way of life. Bob never looked for public praise or attention. For all the good, just, and honorable things Bob did during his life, Bob never thought he was doing anything special—he was simply fulfilling his God-ordained mission of supporting kingdom activity around the world. From Bob's perspective, that was not particularly praiseworthy; he was simply doing what he believed God wanted him to do.

In the late summer of 2010, Bob began to experience some pain in his side and shoulder. In typical Bob fashion, he did not worry about it, did not let it slow him down; but it was there—a nagging pain that would not go away. Into the fall, the pain got a little worse—bad enough to interfere with his golf game. That was my first signal that something was up. Bob did not let too many things get in the way of his golf. We were trying to get one last game in before the season ended, and it did not happen. His last game took place on the Muskoka Lakes Golf Course where he had been a member for over 60 years. He told me he had the course pretty much to himself, and he was pleased to report that he had his best game of the season. He also told me as he walked off the course, he had a strange feeling come over him that this was likely the last golf game he would ever play.

On Sunday, November 21, Bob developed a fever. The fever and the persistent pain were enough for Leslie to insist that Bob get checked out. The ER doctor decided to run some tests and scans, and in the early hours of Monday morning, a visibly shaken doctor told Bob that he had bad news. Bob had stage 4 liver cancer, inoperable and untreatable, and he was given three months to live. The news wasn't just bad, it was shocking. Bob insisted that we not talk about the time frame given him by doctors. He felt strong in spite of the advanced cancer and was confident he would survive well beyond the three months. In one of our post-diagnosis conversations, he told me that he "wanted to live life to the full and plan for the worst." And so, Bob began to put much effort into getting his house in order and at the same time look for treatment options and second opinions. I asked Bob how I could support him, and he said, "Let's make sure we keep meeting as long as we can." And that's what we did.

On the 17th of December, less than four weeks later, I went up to the door of Bob and Leslie's house at 7:45 in the morning—just as I did most Friday mornings. Every previous time, as I knocked on the door I would look through the glass panel of the front door and see Bob standing at the kitchen counter reading the morning paper, waiting for my arrival. This Friday was different—he was not standing but sitting at the kitchen table, not reading, not doing anything—just sitting motionless. This was a strange sight. When I knocked on the door, I watched him get up so very slowly and shuffle to the door. Bob's decline in just a few days was remarkable and overwhelming. I was stunned.

Bob knew things were happening fast, and our conversation quickly turned to what seemed inevitable. He asked whether I would be able to preside over his funeral. In typical Bob fashion, he was thinking more about me than about his quickly approaching death, and he did not want to presume I would be willing or able. In acknowledging our close friendship, he said this funeral would be different and might be too hard on me. I told Bob he was right, this would be really hard for me, but I could not imagine anyone else taking his funeral. He gave me that little half smile that was so typical of Bob. He knew what I would say even before he asked the question. And then we planned his service.

When Leslie came down an hour later, we decided it was time to take Bob to the hospital. He resisted a little, but clearly the fight was gone, and we quietly got ready. When we arrived at the hospital at 10 AM, Bob walked in unassisted, slowly and with considerable effort. By Saturday, he was on heavy pain meds and drifting in and out of sleep. By Sunday, he was having a hard time talking, and on Monday, at mid-afternoon, he was nonresponsive. He died early Tuesday morning.

For someone who ended up so full of cancer, Bob experienced remarkably little suffering. I now see this as a gracious gift to Bob and to us, but he died so quickly his family and friends had a hard time coming to grips with his death.

Three months later, I was on Keat's Island, off the coast of British Columbia, participating in an Arrow Leadership program for emerging leaders. My role as a Leadership Partner provides me the wonderful privilege of working with men and women over a two-year Arrow journey that helps shape them into Christian leaders and servants. During this particular week, the former Arrow President, Carson Pue, was speaking about Soul Friends, and that subject cracked open my grief and sadness. As Carson talked about the need for soul friends, I was overcome by how much I missed Bob, how sad and angry I was. I was also filled with some despair that I might never have another friend like Bob. Given where my head and heart were, I knew I would be useless for a while, so I excused myself and went for a run.

Running on Keat's Island is quite different from running in my home town of Oakville, Ontario. The island affords breathtaking views of mountains and ocean, seals and eagles, ferns and redwoods. It is truly inspiring. But that day, I didn't see any of the beauty—my eyes were filled with tears and my heart kept vacillating between sorrow and anger. I ran hard for a while, trying to exorcise my emotions, but the waves of sadness kept washing over me and the tears kept flowing. I asked God why Bob had to die and what good could possibly come of his sudden passing. I told God that I couldn't make sense of it all and that I missed my friend.

God had me stop by a big tree and look up. The tree was very large in circumference and clearly dominated the surrounding area.

As I looked up, I realized with a bit of a shock that this tree, well over 100 feet tall, was dead. And as I looked at the surrounding canopy, I saw many other trees, not as large, that were very much alive.

Frustrated, I asked God, "Why are you showing me a dead tree?" He said to keep running, and as I ran, he pointed out more deadness—dead trees, old stumps, decaying logs. I did not understand why I was being shown all these dead things. Bob was dead—I understood that—and I angrily suggested that I didn't appreciate the reminders. And then, as I continued running, God directed my attention to a solid, large, very much alive tree—by no means the largest in the forest but substantial, straight, and formidable, and God said to me, "That's you."

Surprised, I stopped and suddenly understood what God was saying. The living trees need all the dead things to grow. The live trees were growing and maturing in the nutrient-rich soil of their dead predecessors. Jesus laid down his life in order to give us the possibility of new life. We who follow Jesus are growing and maturing in the life-giving, gracious soil of his death. The same is also true of Bob. Bob's life, and now his death, does not mark an end to his influence in my life. I continue to draw on the life-giving nutrients provided by his life and death. Those nutrients—the grace that he modeled, the honor and dignity with which he lived his life, the respect he extended to others, the utmost integrity of his character, his passion for missional living, his kingdom world view—will all continue to shape me, form me, fuel me. Bob, like others who live well and die well, provides a nutrient-rich landscape for the living.

Jesus said his death would be good for us. Bob's death, also, is good for me. In the midst of the loss and sadness, a small feeling of excitement rose up in me as I considered what Bob's life and death will yet mean for my future—a much-needed supply of nutrients for a still-maturing spirit hungry for full and abundant life.

CONCLUSION

Understanding Death

Is death something so terrible and absurd that we are better off not thinking or talking about it? Is death such an undesirable part of our existence that we are better off acting as if it were not real? Is death such an absolute end of all our thoughts and actions that we simply cannot face it? Or is it possible to befriend our dying gradually and live open to it, trusting that we have nothing to fear? Is it possible to prepare for our death with the same attentiveness that our parents had in preparing for our birth? Can we wait for our death as for a friend who wants to welcome us home?

—HENRI NOUWEN[42]

SHARON AND I HAVE BEEN MARRIED FOR 39 YEARS, and I am happy to say that we have lived together for all of those years. And yet I regularly surprise Sharon by my presence in our home. I will go into a room where Sharon is going about her business, lost in her thoughts, and all of a sudden Sharon realizes with considerable shock that she is not alone. She jumps six inches off the ground and has a moment of intense fright before she realizes that it's just me. What if, when bumping into death, after that momentary shock, we said, "Oh, it's just you."

It seems rather important to face death before we are in any real danger of doing serious business with death. This requires that we stop ignoring death and instead seek to embrace death. For most of us, just thinking about death, let alone talking about it, is far beyond our comfort zone. And to try to deliberately engage death seems incomprehensible and ludicrous. But embracing our dying may not be as difficult as it first appears. We need a proper understanding of death, and then we need the courage to talk about death. We need to familiarize ourselves with death. Death is as natural as birth and as common as dirt. Death is everywhere, and yet it continues to unsettle us like nothing else can.

Death is that frightening unknown that lurks in the depths of our unconscious mind—like a great shadow that hangs over us. It troubles us, but we have a hard time articulating the trouble. It makes us uneasy but we don't know exactly why. The shadow of death is hard to perceive, but we know it is there, and whenever we bump up against it, it frightens us and we run away and hide.

Talking about death is not morbid nor is it distasteful. It is important and life-giving. The closer one looks at death, the less frightful death becomes. Yes, it is an end, but also a beginning. Yes, there is loss, but also surprising gain. It is sad, and mourning is appropriate and needed, but there is also joy.

One of the reasons we struggle to talk about death is we do not have the knowledge and language to properly discuss it. This conclusion led me to investigate and summarize what the Bible says about death. The Bible is the foremost authority on life and death. I hope you do not simply accept my summary but wrestle with it and use it as a prompt for further study and dialogue. Look up the Bible references for yourself, question the statements, ask God for clarification, discuss these conclusions with your friends, and spend time getting familiar with God's perspective on death.

1. Death is the dissolving of the union between spirit and body. The essence of who we are is not flesh and blood, but spirit. Our body is wonderfully designed and incredibly complex. In Genesis we are told that God created Adam out of the mud of the earth. God fashioned him, like a sculptor moulds the clay. But Adam did not become "alive" until God breathed his Spirit into that lifeless body. For all of our days on this earth, our spirit and body are intricately and necessarily linked. We are body *and* spirit, not one or the other. But upon death, everything changes. The link between body and spirit is temporarily severed. The wonderful container is left behind until the promised resurrection at the end of the age when our bodies will be raised incorruptible. But the spirit breathes new life; released from the earth-bound container, the spirit is now ready to soar to heights and dimensions that are beyond human knowing, that are but hinted at in the Bible, in literature of all kinds, in songs, in poems, and, perhaps most profoundly, in our own hearts. The essence of who we are, our spirit, created in God's image, knows something that our earthly minds simply cannot comprehend. There is more to *life* than we experience here on earth. Death is not the end. We can feel it. (See Genesis 2:7; Ecclesiastes 12:7; 1 Corinthians 15:42-44; James 2:26.)

2. Death is outside God's perfect will for us. That is why we fight death with every fibre of our being. It is, truly, an enemy. It is foreign to us and not at all what we were created for. We have been created for eternity. That is why we find it so hard to conceive of our own death. Death does not make sense and, at a deep level that lies beneath our ability to put into words, we are right. It does not make sense. It was never supposed to be this way. Death is not our destiny. Death is not in the original design of the Creator. Death is an enemy, but an enemy whose sting is gone—an enemy that has been overthrown.

Defanged, still with a fearsome roar, but unable to prevent us from our eternal destiny. (See 1 Corinthians 15:25–26; Romans 6:23; Romans 8:38–39.)

3. *Death is a completely normal part of our lives on Earth.* At times we give death more power than we ought. It is entirely human to die. It is our lot in life. We cannot escape what is inevitable. We will all surely die. Life as we know it carries within itself the seeds of death. This is true of every living organism on planet Earth. Everything dies. (See Hebrews 9:27; Ecclesiastes 3:1–2.)

4. *Our days are limited and we do not know when we will die.* Some die sooner than others. Some might live to see their one-hundredth birthday, but that is rare. There is no way of knowing when we will die, just as there is no way of knowing when Christ will return and establish his kingdom on earth. Only the Father knows. And so, we are to be ready. The biblical concept is that we ought to be living well each and every day, so that at all times we are prepared for the inevitable. (See Psalm 31:15; Psalm 90:10,12; Revelation 1:18.)

5. *Death is the end of our physical life on earth and the continuation of our eternal spiritual life with God.* Death is not some deep dark hole we fall into, never to be seen again, but a doorway to another realm, another dimension. It is like the wardrobe in C. S. Lewis's *The Lion, the Witch and the Wardrobe* that magically transports Peter, Susan, Edmund, and Lucy from wartime England to the strange land of Narnia. It takes us to a new world unlike anything we can comprehend, but one that is filled with God. (See Psalm 23:6; Psalm 73:23–35; 2 Corinthians 4:13–5:10.) No one really knows how this after-death life looks and feels but, in faith, we believe it to be very good. If Jesus himself has gone to prepare a place for us, it has to be good! (See John 14:1–4.)

6. *There is a new heaven and a new earth coming.* At some point in the future, when all things have been dealt with in God's way and in God's time, a new era will begin. John speaks of this in the Bible's final book and calls it a new heaven and new earth (Revelation 21:1). God describes it this way: "God's dwelling place is now among the people, and he will dwell with them. They will be his people, and God himself will be with them and be their God. He will wipe every tear from their eyes. There will be no more death or mourning or crying or pain, for the old order of things has passed away" (Revelation 21:3-4). God is talking about a *real* new heaven and a *real* new earth. We will have new resurrection bodies, and God will literally walk with us on this new earth the way he did with Adam and Eve in the garden. "There will be no more night. They will not need the light of a lamp or the light of the sun, for the Lord God will give them light. And they will reign for ever and ever" (Revelation 22:5).

Talk about death regularly and talk about it in concrete ways, not abstract concepts. Talk about death using the truth of God's Word to guide you. Talk about what we know to be true and leave the rest to God. To be sure, there is mystery here and much we do not know. But we need not fear death. Talking about death will not hasten its coming, but it may well prepare us to receive the many and varied gifts of God's mercy in our season of dying.

ACKNOWLEDGMENTS

My sincere thanks to these:

My long-time friends and colleagues Dr. Arthur Boers and Dr. Rod Wilson, for their incredibly helpful review and insightful suggestions. I am humbled by the many hours they gave to see this book come to print.

Randy Stackaruk for his willingness to read the first draft of each chapter and engage in thoughtful reflection as we sipped caffeinated beverages at The Green Bean.

All who died too soon and in the process taught me about life.

I am particularly grateful for all those who allowed me the privilege of walking with them in their season of dying and for their gracious permission to use their stories. Our collective journeys continue to be a gift to me. In many cases, I started out as a pastor—a giver of care—and somewhere along the journey we became friends. Nowhere is that more true than with Dave and Lorie Moreau, who opened up their lives to me with shocking honesty and vulnerability. My debt to them is larger than I can express. They were the catalysts for this book.

NOTES

1 Henri J.M. Nouwen, *Our Greatest Gift: A Meditation on Dying and Caring* (HarperSanFrancisco, 1994), 14.

2 Nouwen, *Our Greatest Gift*, 16.

3 This is a paraphrase of Nouwen, *Our Greatest Gift*, 67.

4 Douglas Coupland, *Eleanor Rigby* (Toronto: Vintage Canada, 2005), 4.

5 Richard John Neuhaus, in *God With Us: Rediscovering the Meaning of Christmas*, ed. Greg Pennoyer and Gregory Wolfe (Brewster, MA: Paraclete Press, 2007), 31.

6 Sherwin B. Nuland, *How We Die: Reflections on Life's Final Chapter* (New York: Vintage, 1995), 255.

7 Nuland, *How We Die*, 254.

8 Nuland, *How We Die*, 255.

9 Nouwen, *Our Greatest Gift*, 62.

10 Nouwen, *Our Greatest Gift*, 26.

11 Nouwen, *Our Greatest Gift*, 31.

12 Johann Christoph Arnold, *I Tell You a Mystery* (Farmington, PA: Plough, 1996), 68.

13 Arnold, *I Tell You a Mystery*, 32.

14 Chaim Potok, *The Gift of Asher Lev* (New York: Fawcett Crest, 1990), 54.

15 Frederick Buechner, *Godric* (HarperSanFrancisco, 1983), 96.

16 Sarah Young, *Jesus Calling* (Nashville: Thomas Nelson, 2004), February 13 entry.

17 Peter J. Kreeft, *Love Is Stronger Than Death* (San Francisco: Harper and Row, 1979), 69-70.

18 Kathleen Norris, in *God With Us: Rediscovering the Meaning of Christmas*, 105.

19 Fr. Patrick Reardon, *OrthodoxyToday.org*, Oct. 5, 2005, www.orthodoxytoday.org/articles5/ReardonChronos.php.

20 Arthur Paul Boers, *The Way Is Made by Walking: A Pilgrimage Along the Camino de Santiago* (Downer's Grove, IL: InterVarsity, 2007), 134-136.

21 Madeleine L'Engle, *Walking on Water: Reflections on Faith and Art* (New York: Farrar, Straus and Giroux, 2001), 98.

22 Linda Breen Pierce, in *Take Back Your Time: Fighting Overwork and Time Poverty in America*, ed. John de Graaf (San Francisco: Berrett-Koehler Publishers, 2003), 196.

23 Boers, *The Way Is Made by Walking*, 161.

24 Boers, *The Way is Made by Walking*, 179.

25 Kreeft, *Love Is Stronger than Death*, 50.

26 Buechner, *Godric*, 96.

27 Kreeft, *Love Is Stronger Than Death*, 45–46.

28 T. S. Eliot, *The Cocktail Party* (London: Faber and Faber Ltd, 1976), 150.

29 Nouwen, *Our Greatest Gift*, 95.

30 Henri J.M. Nouwen, *The Inner Voice of Love: A Journey Through Anguish to Freedom* (New York: Doubleday, 1998), 107.

31 David Crowder and Mike Hogan, *Everybody Wants to Go to Heaven, but Nobody Wants to Die* (Orlando, FL: Relevant Books, 2006), 177.

32 Alan F. Segal, *Life After Death: A History of the Afterlife in Western Religion* (New York: Random House, 2004), 22.

33 Douglas Coupland, *Eleanor Rigby* (Toronto: Vintage Canada, 2005), Special Features section, 8.

34 Philip Yancey, *Rumors of Another World: What on Earth Are We Missing?* (Grand Rapids, MI: Zondervan, 2003), 219.

35 Leo Tolstoy, *The Death of Ivan Ilyich and Other Stories* (Toronto: Penguin Books, 1960), 129.

36 Frances M. M. Comper, *The Book of the Craft of Dying and Other Early English Tracts Concerning Death* (New York: Arno Press, 1977), 7.

37 Comper, *The Book of the Craft of Dying*, 9.

38 www.deathreference.com/A-Bi/Ars-Moriendi.html

39 These thoughts come from Chapter 3 of *Our Greatest Gift* by Henri Nouwen.

40 Nouwen, *Our Greatest Gift*, xvi–xvii.

41 Luci Shaw, in *God With Us: Rediscovering the Meaning of Christmas*, 96.

42 Nouwen, *Our Greatest Gift*, xii.

BIBLIOGRAPHY

Arnold, Johann Christoph. *I Tell You a Mystery*. Farmington, PA: Plough, 1996.

Boers, Arthur Paul. *The Way Is Made by Walking: A Pilgrimage Along the Camino de Santiago*. Downer's Grove, IL: InterVarsity, 2007.

Buechner, Frederick. *Godric*. HarperSanFrancisco, 1983.

Comper, Frances M. M. *The Book of the Craft of Dying and Other Early English Tracts Concerning Death*. New York: Arno Press, 1977.

Coupland, Douglas. *Eleanor Rigby*. Toronto: Vintage Canada, 2005.

Crowder, David, and Mike Hogan. *Everybody Wants to Go to Heaven but Nobody Wants to Die*. Orlando, FL: Relevant Books, 2006.

Eliot, T. S. *The Cocktail Party*. London: Faber and Faber Ltd, 1976.

Kreeft, Peter J. *Love Is Stronger Than Death*. San Francisco: Harper and Row, 1979.

L'Engle, Madeleine. *Walking on Water: Reflections on Faith and Art*. New York: Farrar, Straus and Giroux, 2001.

Lewis, C. S. *The Lion, the Witch and the Wardrobe*. New York: Scholastic Inc., 1995.

Neuhaus, Richard John. In *God With Us: Rediscovering the Meaning of Christmas*, edited by Pennoyer, Greg and Wolfe, Gregory, Brewster, MA: Paraclete Press, 2007.

Norris, Kathleen. In *God With Us: Rediscovering the Meaning of Christmas*, edited by Pennoyer, Greg and Wolfe, Gregory, Brewster, MA: Paraclete Press, 2007.

Nouwen, Henri J.M. *Our Greatest Gift: A Meditation on Dying and Caring.* HarperSanFrancisco, 1994.

———. *Seeds of Hope.* New York: Doubleday, 1997.

———. *The Inner Voice of Love: A Journey Through Anguish to Freedom.* New York: Doubleday, 1998.

Nuland, Sherwin B., *How We Die: Reflections on Life's Final Chapter.* New York: Vintage, 1995.

Pennoyer, Greg and Gregory Wolfe, ed. *God With Us: Rediscovering the Meaning of Christmas.* Brewster, MA: Paraclete Press, 2007.

Pierce, Linda Breen. In *Take Back Your Time: Fighting Overwork and Time Poverty in America,* edited by John de Graaf. San Francisco: Berrett-Koehler Publishers, 2003.

Potok, Chaim. *The Gift of Asher Lev.* New York: Fawcett Crest, 1990.

Segal, Alan. *Life After Death: A History of the Afterlife in Western Religion.* New York: Random House, 2004.

Shaw, Luci. In *God With Us: Rediscovering the Meaning of Christmas,* edited by Greg Pennoyer and Gregory Wolfe. Brewster, MA: Paraclete Press, 2007.

Tolstoy, Leo. *The Death of Ivan Ilyich and Other Stories.* Toronto: Penguin Books, 1960.

Yancey, Philip. *Rumors of Another World: What on Earth Are We Missing?* Grand Rapids, MI: Zondervan, 2003.

Young, Sarah. *Jesus Calling.* Nashville: Thomas Nelson, 2004.

Young, William P. *The Shack.* Los Angeles, CA: Windblown Media, 2007.

ABOUT PARACLETE PRESS

Paraclete Press is a publisher of books, recordings, and DVDs on Christian spirituality. Our publishing represents a full expression of Christian belief and practice—from Catholic to Evangelical, from Protestant to Orthodox.

We are the publishing arm of the Community of Jesus, an ecumenical monastic community in the Benedictine tradition. As such, we are uniquely positioned in the marketplace without connection to a large corporation and with informal relationships to many branches and denominations of faith.

WHAT WE ARE DOING

Paraclete Press Books

Paraclete publishes books that show the richness and depth of what it means to be Christian. Although Benedictine spirituality is at the heart of who we are and all that we do, we publish books that reflect the Christian experience across many cultures, time periods, and houses of worship. We publish books that nourish the vibrant life of the church and its people.

We have several different series, including the bestselling Paraclete Essentials and Paraclete Giants series of classic texts in contemporary English; Voices from the Monastery—men and women monastics writing about living a spiritual life today; our award-winning Paraclete Poetry series as well as the Mount Tabor Books on the arts; bestselling gift books for children on the occasions of baptism and first communion; and the Active Prayer Series that brings creativity and liveliness to any life of prayer.

Mount Tabor Books

Paraclete's newest series, Mount Tabor Books, focuses on the arts and literature as well as liturgical worship and spirituality, and was created in conjunction with the Mount Tabor Ecumenical Centre for Art and Spirituality in Barga, Italy.

Paraclete Recordings

From Gregorian chant to contemporary American choral works, our recordings celebrate the best of sacred choral music composed through the centuries that create a space for heaven and earth to intersect. Paraclete Recordings is the record label representing the internationally acclaimed choir Gloriæ Dei Cantores, praised for their "rapt and fathomless spiritual intensity" by *American Record Guide*; the Gloriæ Dei Cantores Schola, specializing in the study and performance of Gregorian chant; and the other instrumental artists of the Arts Empowering Life Foundation.

Paraclete Press is also privileged to be the exclusive North American distributor of the recordings of the Monastic Choir of St. Peter's Abbey in Solesmes, France, long considered to be a leading authority on Gregorian chant.

Paraclete Video

Our DVDs offer spiritual help, healing, and biblical guidance for a broad range of life issues including grief and loss, marriage, forgiveness, facing death, bullying, addictions, Alzheimer's, and spiritual formation.

Learn more about us at our website
www.paracletepress.com
Phone us toll-free at 1.800.451.5006

 SCAN TO READ MORE

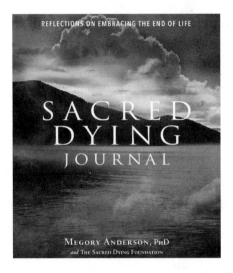

Sacred Dying Journal
Reflections on Embracing the End of Life

Megory Anderson, PhD,
and the Sacred Dying Foundation

ISBN 978-1-64060-007-2 $15.99

Approaching the end of life is a daunting concept, physically, emotionally, and spiritually. This journal gives individuals a place to reflect and express the many thoughts, desires, and discoveries to be made in this special part of life's journey—a blessing for those preparing for life's final stages, and for their loved ones.

Laid out in four sections, the journal includes these headings: Caring for the Body and the Soul, Sacred Dying in Time and Space, Legacies, and Honoring the Body.

My Favorite Color is Blue.
Sometimes.
Roger Hutchison

ISBN 978-1-61261-923-1
$16.99 Paperback

"This original volume belongs in every collection
of books for children about grief."
—Wendy Mogel, PhD, *New York Times* Bestselling author of
The Blessing of a Skinned Knee

The text and illustrations of this lushly colored picture book guide the
reader through different emotions and reactions related to grieving,
including shock, tears, anger, and hope. *My Favorite Color is Blue.
Sometimes.* is for all ages.

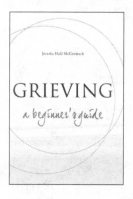

Grieving: A Beginner's Guide
Jerusha Hull McCormack

ISBN 978-1-55725-493-1
$14.99 Paperback

This book is designed to help those in pain—
and specifically those who are coping with how
to grieve the death of a loved one—to imagine
the path before them.

"Chances are, if you are reading this, your heart is broken. This
book is designed to help those in pain—and specifically those who have
lost someone through death—to imagine the path before them. It is
a path of suffering. But it is also a path that may lead to unexpected
discoveries—and to peace." —Jerusha Hull McCormack

Available through your local bookseller
www.paracletepress.com; 1-800-451-5006